THE AUSTRALIAN Women's Weekly
traybakes & slices

THE AUSTRALIAN Women's Weekly

contents

Are traybakes and slices really flat cakes or fat biscuits … or are they something entirely different: a perfect halfway house between the two! When you have to choose between a melting moment or a hazelnut pinwheel, perhaps the most important thing is to make sure you have enough trays to fill the oven. For the perfect slice to munch with your morning cuppa, we have all the sweetest answers!

Pamela Clark

hints for success

To obtain results that look – and taste – as good as ours, read through these guidelines before you start. Our explanations of baking terms and instructions will help you to approach our recipes with confidence and enthusiasm.

Mixing For best results, have butter and eggs at room temperature. Do not overbeat butter and sugar mixtures. Overbeating will result in a mixture which is excessively soft and can cause biscuits to spread too much during baking. Usually, it is best to stir in dry ingredients in two batches, often using a larger bowl.

Overmixed butter and sugar (left) contrasts with correctly beaten mixture (right).

Oven positions Two or more trays of biscuits, or baking tins of slices, can be baked in an oven at the same time provided none of the trays touches the oven sides or door when it is closed. There must be at least a 2cm space around each tray or tin to allow for proper heat circulation and browning.
● For even baking, alternate the position of trays or tins on the oven's shelves halfway through the cooking time. Some ovens have hot spots, so trays or tins need to be rotated too, for even browning.
● As a general rule, the top half of a gas oven will produce the best baking results but, in an electric oven, the lower half is best. Fan-assisted ovens can bake and brown about 4 trays of biscuits at a time without having to alternate shelf positions.

● It is a good idea to check the oven manufacturer's instructions for any particular details that may apply to your oven.

Oven trays and baking tins It is important to use the correct type of oven trays to ensure even baking and browning. We used aluminium trays with quite shallow 'walls' so that the oven heat skimmed over the top of the biscuits, ensuring proper heat circulation and browning.

Piping bags In some recipes, we used a piping bag to force out the mixture; however, only smooth biscuit and cookie mixtures, without any chunky ingredients like nuts or raisins, can be piped.

To test if biscuits are cooked The baking times in this book are based on a minimum cooking time. Every oven differs slightly in temperature, and yours may need testing for accuracy, whether new or old.
● Check biscuits occasionally during baking; opening the oven door briefly will not affect results. Biscuits may look soft in the oven but become firmer or crisp when cold.
● A good way to test that a biscuit is cooked is to push it gently with your finger; if it can be moved on the oven tray without breaking, it is ready to be taken out of the oven.
● Individual recipes instruct when it is necessary to cool on trays or if biscuits should be transferred to racks to cool.

To test if slices are cooked Slices, and bases for layered slices, usually feel slightly soft in the oven but will become firm when cold.

To store biscuits and slices To prevent biscuits and slices from softening, cool completely before storing. Keep biscuits in a container which just holds them: this leaves a minimum of air space but won't crush the contents.
● To avoid softening, biscuits with cream or jam fillings are best assembled just before serving.
● Biscuits and slices will absorb moisture from cakes, bread or scones if stored together, becoming soft in the process.
● If plain biscuits or slices (unfilled and/or un-iced) do soften, place them on oven trays in a single layer and reheat, uncovered, in moderate oven for 5 to 10 minutes to re-crisp; lift onto wire racks to cool.

Biscuit cutters There are many different shapes of cutters available, from cats to Christmas stars to the classic gingerbread man (and don't forget the original simple round cutter!). Use whatever shape suits the recipe and appeals to you as long as it's of a similar dimension to that called for in the individual recipe. We do recommend using metal cutters.

To freeze biscuits and slices Most baked biscuits, cookies and slices can be frozen successfully. However, some icings and cream fillings may crack or change in appearance on thawing.
• Always extract as much air as possible from the container before freezing. Two months is about maximum freezing time. Thawed un-iced and unfilled biscuits will need to be re-crisped, in single layers, on oven trays placed in a moderate oven for between 5 to 10 minutes; cool on wire racks.

what went wrong ...

If biscuits spread on the tray The mixture is too soft due to overbeating; the ingredients have been measured incorrectly; the wrong flour has been used (such as self-raising when plain was called for); the oven was not hot enough to set the mixture quickly.

If biscuits are too hard The ingredients have been measured incorrectly; biscuits have been baked too long or at too high a temperature.

If biscuits are too soft Ingredients have been measured incorrectly; biscuits have not been baked enough or have been softened by steam when stacked on top of one another to cool.

If biscuits are too brown underneath Trays have been over-greased, causing the oven heat to be attracted to the biscuits' bases. Use a pastry brush dipped in a small amount of melted butter to grease trays lightly and evenly. Incorrect oven position and/or temperature could also cause over-browning, as could over-generous measuring, particularly with sweet ingredients like sugar, honey or golden syrup.

Top left: Overbeating causes biscuits (on tray) to spread, unlike correct mixture (on slide).

Bottom left: Over-browning (right) can occur if biscuits have had too much sweetening added.

biscuits

vanilla thins

1 vanilla pod
30g butter, softened
¼ cup (55g) caster sugar
1 egg white, beaten lightly
¼ cup (35g) plain flour

1 Preheat oven to 200°C/180°C fan-assisted. Grease oven trays; line with baking parchment.
2 Halve vanilla pod lengthways; scrape seeds into medium bowl, discard pod. Add butter and sugar to bowl; stir until combined. Stir in egg white and flour.
3 Spoon mixture into piping bag fitted with 5mm plain tube. Pipe 6cm-long strips (making them slightly wider at both ends) about 5cm apart on trays.
4 Bake biscuits about 5 minutes or until edges are browned lightly. Cool on trays.

preparation time 20 minutes
cooking time 5 minutes
makes 24

tip
Vanilla thins can be stored in an airtight container for up to 1 week.

coffee hazelnut meringues

2 egg whites
½ cup (110g) caster sugar
2 teaspoons instant coffee granules
½ teaspoon hot water
3 teaspoons coffee-flavoured liqueur
¼ cup (35g) roasted hazelnuts

1 Preheat oven to 120°C/100°C fan-assisted. Grease oven trays; line with baking parchment.
2 Beat egg whites in small bowl with electric mixer until soft peaks form. Gradually add sugar, beating until dissolved between additions.
3 Meanwhile, dissolve coffee in the water in small jug; stir in liqueur. Fold coffee mixture into meringue mixture.
4 Spoon mixture into piping bag fitted with 5mm fluted tube. Pipe meringues onto trays 2cm apart; top each meringue with a nut.
5 Bake meringues about 45 minutes. Cool in oven with door ajar.

preparation time 10 minutes
cooking time 45 minutes (plus cooling time)
makes 30

tips
Meringues can be stored in an airtight container for up to 3 weeks. Suitable to freeze for up to 3 months.

golden pecan twists

⅓ cup (40g) finely chopped pecans
2 tablespoons golden syrup
125g butter, softened
¼ teaspoon vanilla extract
⅓ cup (75g) caster sugar
1 egg yolk
1 cup (150g) plain flour

1 Preheat oven to 180°C/160°C fan-assisted. Grease oven trays; line with baking parchment.
2 Combine the nuts and half of the golden syrup in a small bowl.
3 Beat butter, extract, sugar, egg yolk and remaining golden syrup in small bowl with electric mixer until light and fluffy. Stir in sifted flour.
4 Shape rounded teaspoons of mixture into balls; roll each ball into 12cm log. Twist each log into a loop, overlapping one end over the other. Place twists on trays 3cm apart; top each twist with ½ teaspoon nut mixture.
5 Bake twists about 10 minutes. Cool on trays.

preparation time 25 minutes
cooking time 10 minutes
makes 30

tips
Twists can be stored in an airtight container for up to 3 weeks. Can be frozen for up to 3 months. Finely chopped macadamias, walnuts or hazelnuts can be used instead of pecans.

honey jumbles

60g butter
½ cup (110g) firmly packed brown sugar
¾ cup (270g) golden syrup
1 egg, beaten lightly
2½ cups (375g) plain flour
½ cup (75g) self-raising flour
½ teaspoon bicarbonate of soda
1 teaspoon ground cinnamon
½ teaspoon ground cloves
2 teaspoons ground ginger
1 teaspoon mixed spice
icing
1 egg white
1½ cups (240g) icing sugar
2 teaspoons plain flour
1 tablespoon lemon juice, approximately
pink food colouring

tip
Jumbles can be stored in an airtight container for up to 1 week.

1 Stir butter, sugar and syrup in medium saucepan over low heat until sugar dissolves; cool 10 minutes. Transfer mixture to large bowl; stir in egg and sifted dry ingredients, in two batches. Knead dough on floured surface until dough loses stickiness. Cover; refrigerate 30 minutes.
2 Preheat oven to 160°C/140°C fan-assisted. Grease oven trays; line with baking parchment.
3 Divide dough into eight portions. Roll each portion into 2cm-thick sausage; cut each sausage into five 6cm lengths. Place about 3cm apart on oven trays; round ends using floured fingers, flatten slightly.
4 Bake biscuits about 15 minutes. Cool on trays.
5 Meanwhile, make icing.
6 Spread jumbles with pink and white icing.
icing Beat egg white lightly in small bowl; gradually stir in sifted icing sugar and flour, then enough juice to make icing spreadable. Place half the mixture in another small bowl; tint with colouring. Keep icings covered with a damp tea towel.

preparation time 10 minutes (plus refrigeration time)
cooking time 15 minutes (plus cooling time)
makes 40

chocolate melting moments

125g butter, softened
2 tablespoons icing sugar
¾ cup (110g) plain flour
2 tablespoons cornflour
1 tablespoon cocoa powder
¼ cup (85g) chocolate hazelnut spread

1 Preheat oven to 180°C/160°C fan-assisted. Grease oven trays; line with baking parchment.
2 Beat butter and sifted icing sugar in small bowl with electric mixer until light and fluffy. Stir in sifted dry ingredients.
3 Spoon mixture into piping bag fitted with 1cm-fluted tube. Pipe stars about 3cm apart on trays.
4 Bake biscuits about 10 minutes. Cool on trays.
5 Sandwich biscuits with hazelnut spread.

preparation time 15 minutes
cooking time 10 minutes (plus cooling time)
makes 20

tip
Melting moments can be stored in an airtight container for up to 1 week.

coconut macaroons

1 egg, separated
1 egg yolk
¼ cup (55g) caster sugar
1⅔ cups (120g) shredded coconut

1 Preheat oven to 150°C/130°C fan-assisted. Grease oven trays; line with baking parchment.
2 Beat egg yolks and sugar in small bowl until creamy; stir in coconut.
3 Beat egg white in small bowl until firm peaks form; stir gently into coconut mixture. Drop heaped teaspoons of the mixture onto trays.
4 Bake macaroons about 15 minutes.
5 Reduce oven to 120°C/100°C fan-assisted; bake further 30 minutes or until biscuits are golden brown. Loosen biscuits while warm; cool on trays.

preparation time 15 minutes
cooking time 45 minutes
makes 18

tips
Macaroons can be stored in an airtight container for up to 3 weeks. Suitable to freeze for up to 3 months.

orange hazelnut butter yoyo bites

250g butter, softened, chopped
1 teaspoon vanilla extract
½ cup (80g) icing sugar
1½ cups (225g) plain flour
½ cup (75g) cornflour
orange hazelnut butter
80g butter, softened
2 teaspoons finely grated orange rind
⅔ cup (110g) icing sugar
1 tablespoon ground hazelnuts

orange hazelnut butter Beat butter, rind and sifted icing sugar in small bowl with electric mixer until light and fluffy. Stir in ground hazelnuts.

1 Preheat oven to 160°C/140°C fan-assisted. Grease oven trays; line with baking parchment.
2 Beat butter, extract and sifted icing sugar in small bowl with electric mixer until light and fluffy; stir in sifted flours, in two batches.
3 Roll rounded teaspoons of mixture into balls; place about 3cm apart on trays. Using fork dusted with flour, press tines gently onto each biscuit to flatten slightly.
4 Bake biscuits about 15 minutes. Cool on trays.
5 Meanwhile, make orange hazelnut butter.
6 Sandwich biscuits with orange hazelnut butter. Serve bites dusted with extra sifted icing sugar, if you like.

preparation time 15 minutes
cooking time 15 minutes (plus cooling time)
makes 20

vanilla kisses

125g butter, softened
½ cup (110g) caster sugar
1 egg
⅓ cup (50g) plain flour
¼ cup (35g) self-raising flour
⅔ cup (100g) cornflour
¼ cup (30g) custard powder
vienna cream
60g butter, softened
½ teaspoon vanilla extract
¾ cup (120g) icing sugar
2 teaspoons milk

1 Preheat oven to 200°C/180°C fan-assisted. Grease oven trays; line with baking parchment.
2 Beat butter, sugar and egg in small bowl with electric mixer until light and fluffy. Stir in sifted dry ingredients, in two batches.
3 Spoon mixture into piping bag fitted with 1cm-fluted tube. Pipe 3cm rosettes about 3cm apart on trays.
4 Bake biscuits about 10 minutes. Cool on trays.
5 Meanwhile, make vienna cream.
6 Sandwich biscuits with vienna cream.
vienna cream Beat butter and extract in small bowl with electric mixer until as white as possible; gradually beat in sifted icing sugar and milk, in two batches.

preparation time 15 minutes
cooking time 10 minutes (plus cooling time)
makes 20

tip
Yoyo bites and Kisses can be stored in an airtight container for up to 1 week.

frangipane jam drops

125g butter, softened
½ teaspoon vanilla extract
½ cup (110g) caster sugar
1 cup (120g) ground almonds
1 egg
⅔ cup (100g) plain flour
2 tablespoons raspberry jam

1   Preheat oven to 180°C/160°C fan-assisted. Grease oven trays; line with baking parchment.
2   Beat butter, extract, sugar and ground almonds in small bowl with electric mixer until light and fluffy. Beat in egg until just combined; stir in sifted flour.
3   Drop level tablespoons of mixture on trays 5cm apart. Use handle of wooden spoon to make small hole (about 1cm deep) in top of each biscuit; fill each hole with ¼ teaspoon jam.
4   Bake jam drops about 15 minutes. Cool on trays.

preparation time 30 minutes
cooking time 15 minutes
makes 24

tips
Jam drops can be stored in an airtight container for up to 3 weeks. Suitable to freeze for up to 3 months.

passionfruit butter yoyo bites

250g butter, softened, chopped
1 teaspoon vanilla extract
½ cup (80g) icing sugar
1½ cups (225g) plain flour
½ cup (75g) cornflour
passionfruit butter
80g butter, softened
⅔ cup (150g) icing sugar
1 tablespoon passionfruit pulp

1   Preheat oven to 160°C/140°C fan-assisted. Grease two oven trays; line with baking parchment.
2   Beat butter, extract and sugar in medium bowl with electric mixer until light and fluffy. Stir in sifted dry ingredients, in two batches.
3   Roll rounded teaspoons of mixture into balls; place on trays about 3cm apart. Using fork dusted with a little flour, press tines gently onto each biscuit to flatten slightly.
4   Bake biscuits about 12 minutes or until firm. Stand on trays 5 minutes; transfer to wire rack to cool.
5   Meanwhile, make passionfruit butter.
6   Sandwich cool biscuits with passionfruit butter.
passionfruit butter   Beat butter and sugar in small bowl with electric mixer until light and fluffy; stir in passionfruit pulp.

preparation time 20 minutes
cooking time 12 minutes (plus cooling time)
makes 37

tip
Yoyo bites can be stored in an airtight container for up to 1 week.

polenta and orange biscuits

125g butter, softened
2 teaspoons finely grated orange rind
⅔ cup (110g) icing sugar
⅓ cup (55g) polenta
1 cup (150g) plain flour

1 Preheat oven to 180°C/160°C fan-assisted. Grease oven trays; line with baking parchment.
2 Beat butter, rind and sifted icing sugar in small bowl with electric mixer until just combined; stir in polenta and sifted flour.
3 Shape mixture into 30cm-rectangular log; cut log into 1cm slices. Place slices on trays 2cm apart.
4 Bake biscuits about 15 minutes. Stand biscuits on trays 5 minutes; transfer to wire rack to cool.

preparation time 15 minutes
cooking time 15 minutes
makes 30

tips
Both biscuits and cookies can be stored in an airtight container for up to 3 weeks. Suitable to freeze for up to 3 months.

maple-syrup butter biscuits

125g butter, softened
½ teaspoon vanilla extract
⅓ cup (80ml) maple syrup
¾ cup (110g) plain flour
¼ cup (35g) cornflour

1 Preheat oven to 180°C/160°C fan-assisted. Grease oven trays; line with baking parchment.
2 Beat butter, extract and maple syrup in small bowl with electric mixer until light and fluffy; stir in sifted flours.
3 Spoon mixture into piping bag fitted with 1cm fluted tube. Pipe stars about 3cm apart onto trays.
4 Bake cookies about 15 minutes. Cool on trays.

preparation time 20 minutes
cooking time 15 minutes
makes 24

white chocolate macadamia cookies

1½ cups (225g) plain flour
½ teaspoon bicarbonate of soda
¼ cup (55g) caster sugar
⅓ cup (75g) firmly packed brown sugar
125g butter, melted
½ teaspoon vanilla extract
1 egg
180g white eating chocolate, chopped coarsely
¾ cup (105g) roasted macadamias,
chopped coarsely

1 Preheat oven to 200°C/180°C fan-assisted. Grease two oven trays; line with baking parchment.
2 Sift flour, soda and sugars into large bowl. Stir in butter, extract and egg then chocolate and nuts.
3 Drop rounded tablespoons of the mixture, 5cm apart on trays.
4 Bake cookies about 10 minutes. Cool on trays.

preparation time 10 minutes
cooking time 10 minutes
makes 24

tips
Both cookies can be stored in an airtight container for up to 3 weeks. Suitable to freeze for up to 3 months.

crunchy muesli cookies

1 cup (90g) rolled oats
1 cup (150g) plain flour
1 cup (220g) caster sugar
2 teaspoons ground cinnamon
¼ cup (35g) dried cranberries
⅓ cup (55g) finely chopped dried apricots
½ cup (70g) slivered almonds
125g butter, chopped coarsely
2 tablespoons golden syrup
½ teaspoon bicarbonate of soda
1 tablespoon boiling water

1 Preheat oven 150°C/130°C fan-assisted. Grease oven trays; line with baking parchment.
2 Combine oats, flour, sugar, cinnamon, dried fruit and nuts in large bowl.
3 Melt butter with golden syrup in small saucepan over low heat; add combined soda and the boiling water. Stir warm butter mixture into dry ingredients.
4 Roll level tablespoons of mixture into balls, place on trays 5cm apart; flatten slightly.
5 Bake cookies about 20 minutes. Cool on trays.

preparation time 15 minutes
cooking time 25 minutes
makes 36

chunky chocolate-candy cookies

125g butter, softened
1 teaspoon vanilla extract
1¼ cups (275g) firmly packed brown sugar
1 egg
1 cup (150g) plain flour
¼ cup (35g) self-raising flour
½ teaspoon bicarbonate of soda
⅓ cup (35g) cocoa powder
½ cup (100g) peanut M&M's
⅓ cup (70g) mini M&M's
75g milk eating chocolate, chopped into chunks

1   Preheat oven to 180°C/160°C fan-assisted. Grease two oven trays; line with baking parchment.
2   Beat butter, extract, sugar and egg in small bowl with electric mixer until smooth (do not overmix). Transfer mixture to large bowl; stir in sifted dry ingredients then all chocolates.
3   Drop level tablespoons of mixture onto trays about 5cm apart.
4   Bake cookies about 10 minutes. Stand cookies on trays 5 minutes; transfer to wire rack to cool.

preparation time 20 minutes
cooking time 10 minutes
makes 36

tips
Cookies can be stored in an airtight container for up to 3 weeks. Suitable to freeze for up to 3 months.

greek-style almond biscuits

3 cups (375g) ground almonds
1 cup (220g) caster sugar
¼ teaspoon almond essence
3 egg whites, beaten lightly
1 cup (80g) flaked almonds

1 Preheat oven to 180°C/160°C fan-assisted. Grease two oven trays; line with baking parchment.
2 Combine ground almonds, sugar and essence in large bowl; stir in egg whites until mixture forms a firm paste.
3 Roll level tablespoons of mixture through nuts; roll into 8cm logs. Shape logs to form crescents. Place crescents on trays.
4 Bake biscuits about 15 minutes. Stand on trays 5 minutes; transfer to wire rack to cool.

preparation time 30 minutes
cooking time 15 minutes
makes 25

tips
Biscuits can be stored in an airtight container for up to 3 weeks. Suitable to freeze for up to 3 months.

fudgy-wudgy chocolate cookies

125g butter, softened
1 teaspoon vanilla extract
1¼ cups (275g) firmly packed brown sugar
1 egg
1 cup (150g) plain flour
¼ cup (35g) self-raising flour
1 teaspoon bicarbonate of soda
⅓ cup (35g) cocoa powder
½ cup (75g) raisins
¾ cup (110g) roasted macadamias, chopped coarsely
½ cup (95g) dark chocolate chips
75g dark eating chocolate, chopped coarsely

1 Preheat oven to 180°C/160°C fan-assisted. Line three oven trays with baking parchment.
2 Beat butter, extract, sugar and egg in medium bowl with electric mixer until smooth. Stir in sifted flours, soda and cocoa powder; stir in raisins, nuts and both chocolates.
3 Drop rounded tablespoons of mixture onto trays about 4cm apart; flatten slightly.
4 Bake cookies 10 minutes. Stand cookies on trays 5 minutes; transfer to wire rack to cool.

preparation time 15 minutes
cooking time 10 minutes
makes 24

almond and redcurrant kisses

60g butter
¼ teaspoon almond essence
¼ cup (55g) caster sugar
¼ cup (30g) ground almonds
⅓ cup (50g) plain flour
1 egg white
⅓ cup redcurrant jelly
icing sugar, for dusting

1 Preheat oven to 180°C/160°C fan-assisted. Line three oven trays with baking parchment.
2 Beat butter, essence and sugar in small bowl with electric mixer until light and fluffy, stir in ground almonds and sifted flour. Beat egg white until soft peaks form, fold into mixture in 2 batches.
3 Drop level teaspoons of mixture about 5cm apart on prepared oven trays. Bake for about 6 minutes or until lightly browned.
4 Lift carefully with spatula onto wire racks to cool. Sandwich biscuits with a little warmed jelly. Dust with sifted icing sugar.

preparation time 15 minutes
cooking time 6 minutes
makes about 20

tips
Cookies can be stored in an airtight container for up to 3 weeks. Suitable to freeze for up to 3 months. Other nuts, such as walnuts or pecans, can be used instead of macadamias.

gingernuts

90g butter
⅓ cup (75g) firmly packed brown sugar
⅓ cup (115g) golden syrup
1⅓ cups (200g) plain flour
¾ teaspoon bicarbonate of soda
1 tablespoon ground ginger
1 teaspoon ground cinnamon
¼ teaspoon ground cloves

1 Preheat oven to 180°C/160°C fan-assisted. Grease oven trays; line with baking parchment.
2 Stir butter, sugar and syrup in medium saucepan over low heat until smooth. Remove from heat; stir in sifted dry ingredients. Cool 10 minutes.
3 Roll rounded teaspoons of mixture into balls. Place about 3cm apart on trays; flatten slightly.
4 Bake biscuits about 10 minutes. Cool on trays.

preparation time 15 minutes
cooking time 10 minutes (plus cooling time)
makes 32

hazelnut pinwheels

1¼ cups (185g) plain flour
100g butter, chopped coarsely
½ cup (110g) caster sugar
1 egg yolk
1 tablespoon milk, approximately
⅓ cup (110g) chocolate hazelnut spread
2 tablespoons ground hazelnuts

1 Process flour, butter and sugar until crumbly. Add egg yolk; process with enough milk until mixture forms a ball. Knead dough on floured surface until smooth; cover, refrigerate 1 hour.
2 Roll dough between sheets of baking parchment to form 20cm x 30cm rectangle; remove top sheet of paper. Spread dough evenly with chocolate hazelnut spread; sprinkle with ground hazelnuts. Using paper as a guide, roll dough tightly from long side to enclose filling. Enclose roll in cling film; refrigerate 30 minutes.
3 Preheat oven to 180°C/160°C fan-assisted. Grease oven trays; line with baking parchment.
4 Remove cling film from dough; cut roll into 1cm slices. Place slices about 2cm apart on trays.
5 Bake biscuits about 20 minutes. Stand biscuits on trays 5 minutes; transfer to wire rack to cool.

preparation time 20 minutes (plus refrigeration time)
cooking time 20 minutes
makes 30

tips
Pinwheels and gingernuts can be stored in an airtight container for up to 3 weeks. Suitable to freeze for up to 3 months.

chunky chewy choc-chip cookies

1 cup (220g) firmly packed brown sugar
½ cup (110g) caster sugar
1½ cups (225g) self-raising flour
½ cup (75g) plain flour
1 cup (150g) coarsely chopped roasted macadamias
185g butter, melted, cooled
1 egg, beaten lightly
1 egg yolk, beaten lightly
2 teaspoons vanilla extract
200g dark eating chocolate, chopped coarsely

1 Preheat oven to 180°C/160°C fan-assisted. Grease oven trays; line with baking parchment.
2 Combine sugars, sifted flours and nuts in large bowl. Add combined butter, egg, egg yolk and extract; mix to a soft dough. Stir in chocolate.
3 Place 2 level tablespoons of biscuit dough on trays about 6cm apart.
4 Bake cookies about 16 minutes or until browned lightly. Cool on trays.

preparation time 25 minutes
cooking time 16 minutes
makes 20

tips
When measuring the dough, we used an ice-cream scoop which was equivalent to two level tablespoons. Cookies can be stored in an airtight container for up to 2 weeks. Suitable to freeze for up to 3 months.

snickerdoodles

250g butter, softened
1 teaspoon vanilla extract
½ cup (110g) firmly packed brown sugar
1 cup (220g) caster sugar
2 eggs
2¾ cups (410g) plain flour
1 teaspoon bicarbonate of soda
½ teaspoon ground nutmeg
1 tablespoon caster sugar, extra
2 teaspoons ground cinnamon

1   Beat butter, extract and sugars in small bowl with electric mixer until light and fluffy. Beat in eggs, one at a time. Transfer mixture to large bowl; stir in combined sifted flour, soda and nutmeg, in two batches. Cover; refrigerate 30 minutes.
2   Preheat oven to 180°C/160°C fan-assisted.
3   Combine extra caster sugar and cinnamon in small shallow bowl. Roll level tablespoons of the dough into balls; roll balls in cinnamon sugar. Place balls 7cm apart on ungreased oven trays.
4   Bake snickerdoodles about 12 minutes. Cool on trays.

preparation time 25 minutes (plus refrigeration time)
cooking time 12 minutes
makes 50

tips
Snickerdoodles can be stored in an airtight container for up to 3 weeks. Suitable to freeze for up to 3 months.

banana, date and rolled oat cookies

125g butter, softened
1 teaspoon finely grated lemon rind
1 cup (220g) firmly packed brown sugar
1 egg yolk
⅓ cup mashed banana
1½ cups (225g) plain flour
½ teaspoon bicarbonate of soda
1 cup (90g) rolled oats
½ cup (75g) finely chopped pitted dried dates
⅔ cup (60g) rolled oats, extra
4 pitted dried dates (35g), chopped coarsely

1 Preheat oven to 180°C/160°C fan-assisted. Grease oven trays; line with baking parchment.
2 Beat butter, rind, sugar and egg yolk in small bowl with electric mixer until combined; stir in banana then sifted flour and soda, oats and dates.
3 Roll level tablespoons of mixture into balls; roll each ball in extra oats then place on trays 5cm apart. Press a piece of coarsely chopped date into centre of each ball.
4 Bake cookies about 15 minutes. Cool on trays.

preparation time 20 minutes
cooking time 15 minutes
makes 28

spicy date and pecan cookies

180g butter
2 teaspoons vanilla essence
½ cup (110g) caster sugar
1 egg yolk
1½ cups (225g) self-raising flour
1 teaspoon ground cinnamon
½ teaspoon ground nutmeg
⅔ cup chopped pitted dried dates
½ cup pecans, chopped
⅔ cup pecan halves

1 Preheat oven to 180°C/160°C fan-assisted. Grease four oven trays.
2 Beat butter, essence, sugar and egg yolk in small bowl with electric mixer until light and fluffy. Stir in sifted flour and spices, then dates and chopped pecans; refrigerate for 30 minutes.
3 Roll rounded teaspoons of mixture into balls, place on prepared oven trays, allowing about 4cm between cookies. Top with pecan halves.
4 Bake for about 12 minutes or until lightly browned; cool on trays.

preparation time 20 minutes (plus refrigeration time)
cooking time 12 minutes
makes about 50

tips
You will need
1 medium overripe
banana (230g) for this
recipe. Biscuits can be
stored in an airtight
container for up to
3 weeks. Suitable to
freeze for up to
3 months.

tips
Biscuits can be stored in an airtight container for up to 3 weeks. Suitable to freeze for up to 3 months.

coffee almond biscuits

1 tablespoon instant coffee granules
3 teaspoons hot water
3 cups (360g) ground almonds
1 cup (220g) caster sugar
2 tablespoons coffee-flavoured liqueur
3 egg whites, beaten lightly
24 coffee beans

1 Preheat oven to 180°C/160°C fan-assisted. Grease oven trays; line with baking parchment.
2 Dissolve coffee in the hot water in large bowl. Add ground almonds, sugar, liqueur and egg whites; stir until mixture forms a firm paste.
3 Roll level tablespoons of mixture into balls, place on trays 3cm apart; flatten slightly. Press coffee beans into tops of biscuits.
4 Bake biscuits about 15 minutes. Cool on trays.

preparation time 15 minutes
cooking time 15 minutes
makes 24

amaretti

1 cup (120g) ground almonds
1 cup (220g) caster sugar
2 egg whites
¼ teaspoon almond essence
20 blanched almonds (20g)

1 Grease two oven trays; line with baking parchment.
2 Beat ground almonds, sugar, egg whites and essence in small bowl with electric mixer for 3 minutes; stand 5 minutes.
3 Spoon mixture into piping bag fitted with 1cm plain tube. Pipe onto trays in circular motion from centre out, to make biscuits about 4cm in diameter. Top each biscuit with a nut. Cover trays of unbaked biscuits loosely with foil; stand at room temperature overnight.
4 Preheat oven to 180°C/160°C fan-assisted.
5 Bake biscuits about 12 minutes. Stand on trays 5 minutes; transfer to wire rack to cool.

preparation time 15 minutes (plus standing time)
cooking time 12 minutes
makes 20

tips
Amaretti can be baked the day they're made, however, they will spread a little more. For best results, stand the amaretti overnight.

tips
Biscuits can be stored in an airtight container for up to 3 weeks. Suitable to freeze for up to 3 months. Use traditional rolled oats for this recipe, not the instant variety.

oat and bran biscuits

1 cup (150g) plain flour
1 cup (60g) unprocessed bran
¾ cup (60g) rolled oats
½ teaspoon bicarbonate of soda
60g chilled butter, chopped
½ cup (110g) caster sugar
1 egg
2 tablespoons water, approximately

1 Process flour, bran, oats, soda and butter until crumbly; add sugar, egg and enough of the water to make a firm dough. Knead dough on floured surface until smooth. Cover; refrigerate 30 minutes.
2 Preheat oven to 180°C/160°C fan-assisted. Grease oven trays; line with baking parchment.
3 Divide dough in half; roll each half between sheets of baking parchment to about 5mm thickness. Cut dough into 7cm rounds; place rounds on trays about 2cm apart.
4 Bake biscuits about 15 minutes. Stand biscuits on trays 5 minutes; transfer to wire rack to cool.

preparation time 15 minutes (plus refrigeration time)
cooking time 15 minutes
makes 30

tips
For a firmer cookie, bake an extra 2 minutes. Cookies can be stored in an airtight container for up to 3 weeks. Suitable to freeze for up to 3 months.

triple-choc cookies

125g butter, softened
½ teaspoon vanilla extract
1¼ cups (250g) firmly packed brown sugar
1 egg
1 cup (150g) plain flour
¼ cup (35g) self-raising flour
1 teaspoon bicarbonate of soda
⅓ cup (35g) cocoa powder
½ cup (85g) chopped raisins
½ cup (95g) milk chocolate chips
75g white eating chocolate, chopped coarsely
75g dark eating chocolate, chopped coarsely

1 Preheat oven to 180°C/160°C fan-assisted. Grease two oven trays; line with baking parchment.
2 Beat butter, extract, sugar and egg in small bowl with electric mixer until smooth; do not overbeat. Stir in sifted dry ingredients, then raisins and all the chocolates.
3 Drop level tablespoons of mixture onto trays about 5cm apart.
4 Bake cookies about 10 minutes. Stand cookies on trays 5 minutes; transfer to wire rack to cool.

preparation time 10 minutes
cooking time 10 minutes
makes 36

chocolate lace crisps

100g dark eating chocolate, chopped coarsely
80g butter, chopped coarsely
1 cup (220g) caster sugar
1 egg
1 cup (150g) plain flour
2 tablespoons cocoa powder
¼ teaspoon bicarbonate of soda
¼ cup (40g) icing sugar

1 Melt chocolate and butter in small saucepan over low heat.
2 Transfer chocolate mixture to medium bowl; stir in caster sugar, egg and sifted flour, cocoa and soda. Cover; refrigerate about 15 minutes or until mixture is firm enough to handle.
3 Preheat oven to 180°C/160°C fan-assisted. Grease oven trays; line with baking parchment.
4 Roll level tablespoons of mixture into balls, roll each ball in icing sugar; place on trays 8cm apart.
5 Bake crisps about 15 minutes. Cool on trays.

preparation time 25 minutes (plus refrigeration time)
cooking time 20 minutes
makes 24

chocolate coffee cream fancies

60g butter
1 teaspoon coffee and chicory essence
1½ tablespoons caster sugar
⅔ cup (100g) plain flour
60g dark eating chocolate, melted
coffee cream
1¼ cups (200g) icing sugar
2 teaspoons oil
¼ teaspoon coffee and chicory essence
1 tablespoon milk, approximately

1 Beat butter, essence and sugar in small bowl with electric mixer until light and fluffy. Stir in sifted flour, mix to a firm dough; cover, refrigerate for 30 minutes.
2 Preheat oven to 180°C/160°C fan-assisted. Grease oven trays. Roll dough between sheets of baking parchment until 3mm thick. Cut 3.5cm rounds from dough, place rounds about 2cm apart on oven trays.
3 Bake for about 8 minutes or until lightly coloured. Stand biscuits for a few minutes on trays, lift onto wire rack to cool.
4 Spread biscuits with coffee cream, stand on wire rack until set. Pipe or drizzle biscuits with melted chocolate.
coffee cream Sift icing sugar into bowl, stir in oil, essence and enough milk to make spreadable.

preparation time 15 minutes (plus refrigeration time)
cooking time 8 minutes
makes about 40

tip
Biscuits can be stored in an airtight container for up to 1 week.

almond crisps

125g butter, softened
¼ cup (55g) caster sugar
1 cup (150g) self-raising flour
¼ cup (30g) ground almonds
2 tablespoons flaked almonds

1 Preheat oven to 200°C/180°C fan-assisted. Grease oven trays; line with baking parchment.
2 Beat butter and sugar in small bowl with electric mixer until smooth. Stir in flour and ground almonds.
3 Roll level tablespoons of mixture into balls; place onto trays about 5cm apart. Flatten slightly with a floured fork to 1cm thick; sprinkle with flaked almonds.
4 Bake crisps about 10 minutes or until browned. Stand crisps on trays 5 minutes; transfer to wire racks to cool.

preparation time 25 minutes
cooking time 10 minutes
makes 15

tip
Almond crisps can be stored in an airtight container for up to 2 weeks.

passionfruit creams

1 cup (150g) plain flour
½ cup (75g) self-raising flour
2 tablespoons cornflour
2 tablespoons custard powder
⅔ cup (100g) icing sugar
90g butter
1 egg yolk
¼ cup passionfruit pulp
passionfruit cream
¼ cup (55g) caster sugar
1 tablespoon water
60g unsalted butter
1 tablespoon passionfruit pulp

1 Sift dry ingredients into bowl, rub in butter. Add egg yolk and passionfruit pulp, mix to a firm dough. Turn dough onto lightly floured surface, knead lightly until smooth; cover, refrigerate for 30 minutes.
2 Preheat oven to 200°C/180°C fan-assisted. Grease oven trays.
2 Roll dough between sheets of baking parchment until 3mm thick. Cut 5.5cm rounds from dough. Place on oven trays, allowing about 3cm between biscuits.
3 Bake for about 15 minutes or until lightly browned. Cool on wire racks.
4 Spoon passionfruit cream into piping bag fitted with small fluted tube, pipe cream onto each biscuit. Dust with sifted icing sugar, if desired.

passionfruit cream Combine sugar and water in pan, stir over heat until sugar is dissolved. Bring to boil, simmer for 2 minutes; cool. Beat butter in small bowl with electric mixer until light and fluffy, gradually add cold sugar syrup, beat well between each addition. Stir in passionfruit pulp.

preparation time 25 minutes (plus refrigeration time)
cooking time 15 minutes
makes about 35

almond and chocolate florentines

50g butter
¼ cup (55g) caster sugar
2 teaspoons honey
1 tablespoon plain flour
1 tablespoon double cream
½ cup (40g) flaked almonds
50g dark eating chocolate, melted

1 Preheat oven to 200°C/180°C fan-assisted. Grease four oven trays; line with baking parchment.
2 Combine butter, sugar, honey, flour and cream in small saucepan; bring to the boil, stirring. Reduce heat; cook, without stirring, 2 minutes. Remove from heat; stir in nuts.
3 Drop level teaspoons of mixture about 8cm apart onto oven trays.
4 Bake florentines about 6 minutes or until golden brown. Remove from oven; using metal spatula, push florentines into rounds. Cool on trays 1 minute then carefully lift florentines onto baking-paper-covered wire rack to cool.
5 Drizzle florentines with chocolate; refrigerate until set.

preparation time 20 minutes (plus refrigeration time)
cooking time 6 minutes (plus cooling time)
makes 28

> **tip**
> Florentines can be stored in an airtight container for up to 2 weeks. Not suitable to freeze.

florentines

¾ cup (120g) sultanas
2 cups (60g) cornflakes
¾ cup unsalted roasted peanuts, chopped
½ cup chopped red glacé cherries
⅔ cup (165ml) sweetened condensed milk
150g dark eating chocolate, melted

1 Preheat oven to 180°C/160°C fan-assisted. Grease oven trays; line with baking parchment.
2 Combine sultanas, cornflakes, peanuts, cherries and milk in bowl; mix well.
3 Place 1½-tablespoon portions of mixture about 5cm apart on prepared oven trays.
4 Bake about 10 minutes or until lightly browned; cool on trays.
5 Spread base of each biscuit with chocolate. Make wavy lines in chocolate with fork just before chocolate sets.

preparation time 15 minutes
cooking time 10 minutes (plus cooling time)
makes about 18

gingerbread kids

125g butter, chopped
⅓ cup (75g) firmly packed brown sugar
½ cup (175g) golden syrup
3 cups (450g) plain flour
2 teaspoons ground ginger
2 teaspoons ground cinnamon
½ teaspoon ground cloves
2 teaspoons bicarbonate of soda
1 egg, beaten lightly
1 teaspoon vanilla extract
royal icing
1 egg white
1 cup (160g) icing sugar
food colourings

tips
If the mixture in step 3 is dry and crumbly, add a little more beaten egg. You can use any shape of cutter for this recipe. Biscuits can be stored in an airtight container for up to 3 weeks. Uniced biscuits suitable to freeze for up to 3 months.

1   Preheat oven to 180°C/160°C fan-assisted. Grease oven trays; line with baking parchment.
2   Stir butter, sugar and golden syrup in small saucepan over low heat until butter has melted. Remove from heat; cool 5 minutes.
3   Sift combined flour, spices and soda into large bowl; stir in butter mixture, egg and extract.
4   Knead dough lightly on floured surface; roll dough to 5mm thickness. Using gingerbread-man cutter, cut out shapes; place on trays.
5   Bake gingerbread kids about 10 minutes or until golden brown. Cool on trays.
6   Meanwhile, make royal icing. Decorate gingerbread kids as you like with royal icing.
royal icing   Beat egg white in small bowl with electric mixer until just frothy; gradually add sifted icing sugar, beating between additions, until stiff peaks form. Tint with food colourings as desired.

preparation time 30 minutes
cooking time 10 minutes (plus cooling time)
makes 20

anzac biscuits

1 cup (90g) rolled oats
1 cup (150g) plain flour
1 cup (220g) caster sugar
¾ cup (60g) desiccated coconut
125g butter, chopped
1 tablespoon golden syrup
1½ teaspoons bicarbonate of soda
2 tablespoons boiling water

1 Preheat oven to 150°C/130°C fan-assisted. Grease oven trays; line with baking parchment.
2 Combine oats, flour, sugar and coconut in large bowl.
3 Stir butter and syrup in small saucepan over low heat until smooth.
4 Combine soda and the boiling water in a small heatproof bowl, add to butter mixture; stir into dry ingredients while warm.
5 Place level tablespoons of mixture onto trays about 5cm apart; press lightly.
6 Bake biscuits about 25 minutes. Loosen biscuits while warm; cool on trays.

preparation time 30 minutes
cooking time 25 minutes
makes 25

tip
Biscuits can be stored in an airtight container for up to 2 weeks.

anise-flavoured shortbread

250g butter, softened
½ cup (80g) icing sugar
2 cups (300g) plain flour
½ cup (100g) rice flour
3 teaspoons ground aniseed

1   Beat butter and sifted icing sugar in medium bowl with electric mixer until light and fluffy. Add sifted flours and aniseed, in two batches, beating on low speed after each addition, only until combined. Knead on floured surface until smooth. Cover; refrigerate 1 hour.
2   Preheat oven to 160°C/140°C fan-assisted. Grease three oven trays; line with baking parchment.
3   Roll dough between sheets of baking parchment until 5mm thick. Cut 36 x 6cm flower shapes or rounds from dough; place on oven trays about 3cm apart. Refrigerate 15 minutes.
4   Bake biscuits about 12 minutes. Cool on trays.

preparation time 20 minutes (plus refrigeration time)
cooking time 12 minutes
makes 36

tips
Shortbreads can be stored in an airtight container for up to 3 weeks. Suitable to freeze for up to 3 months.

traditional shortbread

250g butter, softened
⅓ cup (75g) caster sugar
1 tablespoon water
2 cups (300g) plain flour
½ cup (100g) rice flour
2 tablespoons white sugar

1 Preheat oven to 160°C/140°C fan-assisted. Grease two oven trays.
2 Beat butter and caster sugar in medium bowl with electric mixer until light and fluffy; stir in the water and sifted flours, in two batches. Knead on floured surface until smooth.
3 Divide mixture in two portions; shape each portion, on separate trays, into 20cm rounds. Mark each round into 12 wedges; prick with fork. Pinch edges of rounds with fingers; sprinkle with white sugar.
4 Bake shortbread about 40 minutes. Stand on trays 5 minutes. Using sharp knife, cut into wedges along marked lines. Cool on trays.

preparation time 20 minutes
cooking time 40 minutes
makes 24

VARIATIONS

lemon squares Beat 1 tablespoon finely grated lemon rind into the butter and sugar mixture. Shape dough into a 30cm x 4cm rectangular log, cut into 1cm slices. Place about 3cm apart on oven trays; sprinkle with 2 tablespoons raw sugar. Bake about 20 minutes. Stand 5 minutes; place onto wire racks to cool. **makes** 24

white chocolate and nut mounds Roast ½ cup unsalted pistachios; chop two-thirds finely, reserve remainder. Fold chopped nuts and 100g finely chopped white chocolate into basic shortbread mixture before flours are added. Shape level tablespoons of mixture into mounds; place 3cm apart on oven trays, press a reserved nut into each mound. Bake 20 minutes. Stand 5 minutes; place onto wire racks to cool. Serve dusted with icing sugar. **makes** 32

lemon shortbreads

250g butter, softened, chopped
1 teaspoon finely grated lemon rind
⅓ cup (55g) icing sugar
1½ cups (225g) plain flour
½ cup (75g) cornflour
½ cup (85g) mixed peel, chopped finely

1 Preheat oven to 180°C/160°C fan-assisted. Grease oven trays.
2 Beat butter, rind and sifted icing sugar in small bowl with electric mixer until just changed in colour. Stir in sifted flours, in two batches.
3 Place mixture into large piping bag fitted with fluted tube, pipe mixture into rosettes, about 2cm apart, onto trays; sprinkle with mixed peel.
4 Bake biscuits about 15 minutes or until browned lightly. Stand biscuits on tray 10 minutes; transfer to wire racks to cool.

preparation time 20 minutes
cooking time 15 minutes
makes 40

tips
Shortbread can be
stored in an airtight
container for up to
3 weeks. Suitable to
freeze for up to
3 months.

macadamia shortbread

250g butter, softened, chopped
½ cup (110g) caster sugar
2 teaspoons vanilla extract
2 cups (300g) plain flour
½ cup (75g) rice flour
½ cup (75g) finely chopped macadamias
2 tablespoons caster sugar, extra

1 Preheat oven to 160°C/140°C fan-assisted. Grease two oven trays.
2 Beat butter, sugar and extract in small bowl with electric mixer until pale and fluffy. Transfer mixture to large bowl; stir in sifted flours and nuts, in two batches. Knead on floured surface until smooth.
3 Divide mixture into two portions; roll each portion, between sheets of baking parchment, into 23cm circle. Press an upturned 22cm loose-based fluted flan tin into shortbread to cut rounds. Cut each round into 12 wedges. Place on trays; mark with a fork, sprinkle with extra sugar.
4 Bake shortbread about 20 minutes or until a pale straw colour. Stand on tray 10 minutes; transfer to wire rack to cool.

preparation time 20 minutes
cooking time 20 minutes (plus cooling time)
makes 24

tips
Shortbread can be stored in an airtight container for up to 3 weeks. Suitable to freeze for up to 3 months.

pistachio shortbread mounds

⅔ cup (90g) roasted pistachios
250g butter, softened
1 cup (160g) icing sugar
1½ cups (225g) plain flour
2 tablespoons rice flour
2 tablespoons cornflour
¾ cup (90g) ground almonds
⅓ cup (55g) icing sugar, extra

1 Preheat oven to 150°C/130°C fan-assisted. Grease two oven trays; line with baking parchment.
2 Coarsely chop half the nuts; leave the remaining nuts whole.
3 Beat butter and sugar in small bowl with electric mixer until light and fluffy. Transfer mixture to large bowl; stir in sifted flours, ground almonds and chopped nuts.
4 Shape level tablespoons of mixture into mounds; place on trays about 3cm apart. Press one whole nut on each mound.
5 Bake mounds about 25 minutes or until firm. Stand mounds on trays 5 minutes; transfer to wire rack to cool. Serve mounds dusted with extra sifted icing sugar.

preparation time 25 minutes
cooking time 25 minutes
makes 35

tips
Shortbread can be stored in an airtight container for up to 3 weeks. Suitable to freeze for up to 3 months.

pistachio and cranberry biscotti

60g butter, softened
1 teaspoon vanilla extract
1 cup (220g) caster sugar
2 eggs
1¾ cups (260g) plain flour
½ teaspoon bicarbonate of soda
1 cup (130g) dried cranberries
¾ cup (110g) coarsely chopped roasted pistachios
1 egg, extra
1 tablespoon water
2 tablespoons caster sugar, extra

1 Beat butter, extract and sugar in medium bowl until combined. Beat in eggs, one at a time. Stir in sifted flour and soda then cranberries and nuts. Cover dough; refrigerate 1 hour.
2 Preheat oven to 180°C/160°C fan-assisted. Grease oven tray.
3 Knead dough on floured surface until smooth but still sticky. Halve dough; shape each half into 30cm log. Place logs on oven tray.
4 Combine extra egg with the water in small bowl. Brush egg mixture over logs; sprinkle with extra sugar.
5 Bake logs about 20 minutes or until firm; cool 3 hours or overnight.
6 Preheat oven to 150°C/130°C fan-assisted.
7 Using serrated knife, cut logs diagonally into 1cm slices. Place slices, in single layer, on ungreased oven trays. Bake about 15 minutes or until dry and crisp, turning halfway through cooking time; transfer to wire racks to cool.

preparation time 20 minutes (plus refrigeration time)
cooking time 40 minutes (plus cooling time)
makes 60

tip
Biscotti can be stored in an airtight container for up to 4 weeks.

white choc, apple and almond bread

3 egg whites
⅓ cup (75g) caster sugar
¾ cup (110g) plain flour
¼ teaspoon ground cinnamon
⅔ cup (110g) whole blanched almonds
1 cup (55g) finely chopped dried apples
50g white eating chocolate, melted

tip
Almond bread can be stored in an airtight container for up to 4 weeks.

1 Preheat oven to 180°C/160°C fan-assisted. Grease 8cm x 26cm shallow cake tin; line base and two long sides with baking parchment, extending paper 5cm over edges.
2 Beat egg whites and sugar in small bowl with electric mixer until sugar dissolves. Fold in sifted flour then cinnamon, nuts and apple. Spread mixture into tin.
3 Bake bread about 30 minutes. Stand bread in tin 10 minutes; turn, top-side up, onto wire rack to cool.
4 Reduce oven temperature to 150°C/130°C fan-assisted.
5 Using serrated knife, slice cooled bread thinly; place slices on ungreased oven trays. Bake about 15 minutes or until crisp. Turn onto wire rack to cool. Drizzle biscuits with chocolate.

preparation time 10 minutes
cooking time 1 hour (plus cooling time)
makes 50

hazelnut biscotti

1⅓ cups (200g) plain flour
⅓ cup (50g) self-raising flour
1 cup (220g) caster sugar
2 eggs, beaten lightly
½ cup (75g) roasted hazelnuts
1 teaspoon vanilla extract

1 Preheat oven to 180°C/160°C fan-assisted. Grease oven tray.
2 Sift flours and sugar into large bowl. Stir in egg, nuts and extract until mixture becomes a firm dough.
3 Knead dough on floured surface until mixture just comes together; shape mixture into 25cm log, place on tray.
4 Bake log about 35 minutes or until firm. Cool on tray.
5 Reduce oven temperature to 150°C/130°C fan-assisted.
6 Using a serrated knife, cut log diagonally into 5mm slices. Place slices, in single layer, on ungreased oven trays. Bake about 10 minutes or until dry and crisp, turning over halfway through cooking; transfer to wire racks to cool.

preparation time 40 minutes
cooking time 45 minutes (plus cooling time)
makes 50

tip
Biscotti can be stored in an airtight container for up to 4 weeks.

apricot and pine nut biscotti

2 eggs
1¼ cups (275g) caster sugar
1 teaspoon vanilla extract
1½ cups (225g) plain flour
½ cup (75g) self-raising flour
½ cup (125g) coarsely chopped glacé apricots
¼ cup (40g) roasted pine nuts
2 teaspoons water

1 Preheat oven to 180°C/160°C fan-assisted. Grease oven tray.
2 Whisk eggs, sugar and extract in medium bowl. Stir in sifted flours, apricots, pine nuts and the water; mix to a sticky dough. Knead dough on floured surface until smooth.
3 Divide dough into two portions. Using floured hands, roll each portion into a 30cm log. Place logs on tray.
4 Bake logs about 25 minutes. Cool on tray 10 minutes.
5 Reduce oven to 150°C/130°C fan-assisted.
6 Using a serrated knife, cut logs diagonally into 1cm slices. Place slices, in single layer, on ungreased oven trays. Bake about 25 minutes or until dry and crisp, turning over halfway through cooking; transfer to wire racks to cool.

preparation time 25 minutes
cooking time 50 minutes (plus cooling time)
makes 60

choc nut biscotti

2 eggs
1 cup (220g) caster sugar
1⅔ cups (250g) plain flour
1 teaspoon baking powder
1 cup (150g) roasted pistachios
½ cup (70g) slivered almonds
¼ cup (25g) cocoa powder

1   Preheat oven to 180°C/160°C fan-assisted. Grease oven tray.
2   Whisk eggs and sugar in medium bowl. Stir in sifted flour, baking powder and nuts; mix to a sticky dough.
3   Knead dough on floured surface until smooth. Divide dough into two portions. Using floured hands, knead one portion on floured surface until smooth, but still slightly sticky. Divide this portion into four pieces; roll each piece into 25cm log shape.
4   Knead cocoa into remaining portion of dough until smooth. Divide chocolate dough into two pieces; roll each piece into 25cm log shape.
5   Place one chocolate log on tray. Place a plain log on each side, press gently together to form a slightly flattened shape. Repeat with remaining logs.
6   Bake logs about 30 minutes. Cool on tray 10 minutes.
7   Reduce oven to 150°C/130°C fan-assisted.
8   Using a serrated knife, cut logs diagonally into 5mm slices. Place slices, in single layer, on ungreased oven trays. Bake about 20 minutes or until dry and crisp, turning over halfway through cooking; transfer to wire racks to cool.

preparation time 35 minutes
cooking time 50 minutes (plus cooling time)
makes 100

orange, coconut and almond biscotti

2 eggs
1 cup (220g) caster sugar
1 teaspoon grated orange rind
1⅓ cups (200g) plain flour
⅓ cup (50g) self-raising flour
⅔ cup (50g) shredded coconut
1 cup (160g) blanched almonds

1 Preheat oven to 180°C/160°C fan-assisted. Grease oven tray.
2 Whisk eggs, sugar and rind together in medium bowl. Stir in sifted flours, coconut and nuts; mix to a sticky dough.
3 Knead dough on floured surface until smooth. Divide dough into two portions. Using floured hands, roll each portion into a 20cm log; place logs on tray.
4 Bake logs about 35 minutes. Cool on tray 10 minutes.
5 Reduce oven to 150°C/130°C fan-assisted.
6 Using a serrated knife, cut logs diagonally into 1cm slices. Place slices, in single layer, on ungreased oven trays. Bake about 25 minutes or until dry and crisp, turning over halfway through cooking; transfer to wire racks to cool.

preparation time 25 minutes
cooking time 1 hour (plus cooling time)
makes 40

tip
Biscotti can be stored in an airtight container for up to 4 weeks.

slices

tangy lemon squares

125g butter, softened
¼ cup (40g) icing sugar
1¼ cups (185g) plain flour
3 eggs
1 cup (220g) caster sugar
2 teaspoons finely grated lemon rind
½ cup (125ml) lemon juice

tips
Look for lemons that are bright and heavy - they have more juice and flavour. This slice can be stored, covered, in the refrigerator for up to 3 days.

1 Preheat oven to 180°C/160°C fan-assisted. Grease 23cm-square shallow cake tin; line base with baking parchment, extending the paper 5cm above two opposite sides.
2 Beat butter and icing sugar in small bowl with electric mixer until smooth. Stir in 1 cup (150g) of the flour. Press mixture over base of tin.
3 Bake about 15 minutes or until browned lightly.
4 Meanwhile, whisk eggs, caster sugar, remaining flour, rind and juice in bowl until combined; pour over hot base.
5 Bake slice further 20 minutes or until firm. Cool in tin, on wire rack, before cutting. Dust with extra sifted icing sugar, if you like.

preparation time 20 minutes
cooking time 35 minutes (plus cooling time)
makes 16

no-bowl chocolate nut slice

90g butter, melted
1 cup (100g) digestive biscuit crumbs
1½ cups (285g) dark chocolate chips
1 cup (70g) shredded coconut
1 cup (140g) crushed mixed nuts
395g can sweetened condensed milk

1   Preheat oven to 180°C/160°C fan-assisted. Grease 23cm-square shallow cake tin; line base with baking parchment extending paper 5cm over two opposite sides.
2   Pour butter into tin; sprinkle evenly with biscuit crumbs, chocolate chips, coconut and nuts. Drizzle with condensed milk.
3   Bake slice about 30 minutes. Cool in tin before cutting into pieces.

preparation time 10 minutes
cooking time 30 minutes (plus cooling time)
makes about 18

tip
This slice can be stored, covered, in the refrigerator for up to 1 week.

choc-cherry macaroon slice

3 egg whites
½ cup (110g) caster sugar
100g dark eating chocolate, grated coarsely
¼ cup (35g) plain flour
1⅓ cups (95g) shredded coconut, toasted
¾ cup (150g) glacé cherries, chopped coarsely
50g dark eating chocolate, melted

1   Preheat oven to 150°C/130°C fan-assisted. Grease 19cm x 29cm baking tin; line with baking parchment, extending paper 5cm over long sides.
2   Beat egg whites in small bowl with electric mixer until soft peaks form; gradually add sugar, beating until dissolved between additions. Fold in grated chocolate, flour, coconut and cherries. Spread mixture into tin.
3   Bake slice about 45 minutes. Cool in tin.
4   Drizzle slice with melted chocolate; refrigerate until set before cutting into slices.

preparation time 15 minutes
cooking time 45 minutes (plus cooling and refrigeration time)
makes 16

chocolate hazelnut slice

250g plain chocolate biscuits
60g butter, melted
4 eggs, separated
¾ cup (165g) caster sugar
½ cup (50g) ground hazelnuts
2 tablespoons plain flour
1 tablespoon cocoa powder
topping
125g butter, softened
½ cup (110g) caster sugar
1 tablespoon orange juice
200g dark eating chocolate, melted

1 Preheat oven to 180°C/160°C fan-assisted. Grease 20cm x 30cm shallow baking tin; line base with baking parchment, extending paper 5cm over long sides.
2 Process biscuits until fine. Combine 1 cup of the biscuit crumbs with butter in medium bowl; press over base of tin. Refrigerate 10 minutes.
3 Beat egg whites in small bowl with electric mixer until soft peaks form. Gradually add sugar, beating until dissolved between additions; fold in ground hazelnuts, remaining biscuit crumbs and flour. Spread mixture over biscuit base.
4 Bake slice 20 minutes. Cool in tin 20 minutes.
5 Reduce oven to 170°C/150°C fan-assisted.
6 Meanwhile, make topping; spead over slice.
7 Bake slice further 20 minutes. Cool in tin. Refrigerate until firm; dust with sifted cocoa before cutting.
topping Beat butter, sugar, egg yolks and juice in small bowl with electric mixer until light and fluffy. Stir in cooled chocolate.

preparation time 30 minutes
cooking time 40 minutes (plus cooling and refrigeration time)
makes 24

fruit chews

90g butter, chopped coarsely
⅓ cup (75g) firmly packed brown sugar
1¼ cups (185g) plain flour
1 egg yolk
topping
2 eggs
1 cup (220g) firmly packed brown sugar
⅓ cup (50g) self-raising flour
½ cup (85g) coarsely chopped raisins
¾ cup (120g) sultanas
1¼ cups (185g) roasted unsalted peanuts
1 cup (90g) desiccated coconut

1 Preheat oven to 180°C/160°C fan-assisted. Grease 20cm x 30cm shallow baking tin; line base with baking parchment, extending paper 5cm over long sides.
2 Stir butter and sugar in medium saucepan over medium heat until butter is melted. Stir in sifted flour and egg yolk. Press mixture over base of tin.
3 Bake about 10 minutes or until browned lightly; cool.
4 Meanwhile, make topping; spread over cold base.
5 Bake slice about 30 minutes. Cool in tin before cutting.
topping Beat eggs and sugar in small bowl with electric mixer until changed to a paler colour and thickened slightly; stir in sifted flour. Transfer mixture to medium bowl; stir in remaining ingredients.

preparation time 15 minutes
cooking time 40 minutes (plus cooling time)
makes 18

tips
Brown sugar gives this nutty slice the colour and taste of caramel. This slice can be stored in an airtight container for up to 1 week.

fruity almond pistachio slice

¾ cup (180ml) sweetened condensed milk
125g butter, chopped
2 teaspoons grated lemon rind
1½ cups (150g) digestive biscuit crumbs
½ cup (125g) coarsely chopped red glacé cherries
½ cup (150g) coarsely chopped glacé figs
½ cup (125g) coarsely chopped glacé peaches
⅓ cup (55g) coarsely chopped roasted almonds
⅓ cup (50g) coarsely chopped roasted pistachios
¾ cup (65g) desiccated coconut
100g dark eating chocolate, melted
60g butter, melted, extra
1 tablespoon coarsely chopped roasted
almonds, extra
1 tablespoon coarsely chopped roasted
pistachios, extra

1 Grease 19cm x 29cm baking tin; line base with baking
parchment, extending paper 5cm over long sides.
2 Stir condensed milk, butter and rind in medium
saucepan over heat until butter is melted. Stir in biscuit
crumbs, fruit, nuts and coconut. Press mixture evenly over
base of tin.
3 Spread with combined chocolate and extra butter,
sprinkle with extra nuts; refrigerate until set.

preparation time 35 minutes
cooking time 5 minutes (plus refrigeration time)
makes about 24

tip
This slice can be
stored, covered,
in the refrigerator
for up to 1 week.

sweet coconut slice

1 cup (150g) plain flour
½ cup (75g) self-raising flour
2 tablespoons caster sugar
125g chilled butter, chopped
1 egg
1 tablespoon iced water
½ cup (160g) apricot jam
10 red glacé cherries, halved
coconut filling
1 cup (220g) caster sugar
1 cup (250ml) water
3½ cups (280g) desiccated coconut
3 eggs, beaten lightly
60g butter, melted
¼ cup (60ml) milk
1 teaspoon vanilla extract
1 teaspoon baking powder

1 Process flours, sugar and butter until combined.
Add egg and the water, process until mixture forms a ball;
cover, refrigerate 30 minutes.
2 Meanwhile, make coconut filling.
3 Preheat oven to 180°C/160°C fan-assisted. Line 25cm
x 30cm swiss roll tin with baking parchment, extending
paper 5cm over long sides.
4 Roll pastry between sheets of baking parchment until
3mm thick and large enough to cover base of tin. Gently
ease into base of tin.
5 Brush jam evenly over pastry base. Spread coconut
mixture over jam. Place cherry halves evenly over slice top.
6 Bake slice about 35 minutes. Cool in tin before cutting
into slices.
coconut filling Stir sugar and the water in small
saucepan over heat until sugar is dissolved. Bring to the
boil; boil 3 minutes without stirring. Cool 5 minutes. Place
coconut in large bowl, stir in sugar syrup, egg, butter, milk,
extract and baking powder.

preparation time 40 minutes (plus refrigeration time)
cooking time 40 minutes (plus cooling time)
makes 20

tips
This slice can be
stored in an airtight
container for up to 4 days.
Cooked slice is suitable
to freeze, covered, for
up to 2 weeks. Thaw at
room temperature.

lemon meringue slice

90g butter, softened
2 tablespoons caster sugar
1 egg
1 cup (150g) plain flour
¼ cup (80g) apricot jam
lemon topping
2 eggs
2 egg yolks
½ cup (110g) caster sugar
300ml double cream
1 tablespoon finely grated lemon rind
2 tablespoons lemon juice
meringue
3 egg whites
¾ cup (165g) caster sugar

1 Preheat oven to 200°C/180°C fan-assisted. Grease 19cm x 29cm baking tin; line base with baking parchment, extending paper 5cm over long sides.
2 Beat butter, sugar and egg in small bowl with electric mixer until pale in colour; stir in sifted flour, in two batches. Press dough over base of tin; prick dough all over lightly with a fork.
3 Bake about 15 minutes or until browned lightly. Cool 20 minutes; spread base with jam.
4 Reduce oven temperature to 170°C/150°C fan-assisted.
5 Make lemon topping; pour over base. Bake about 35 minutes or until set; cool 20 minutes. Roughen surface of topping with fork.
6 Increase oven temperature to 220°C/200°C fan-assisted.
7 Make meringue; spread evenly over topping.
8 Bake slice 3 minutes or until browned lightly. Cool in tin 20 minutes before cutting.
lemon topping Whisk ingredients together in medium bowl until combined.
meringue Beat egg whites in small bowl with electric mixer until soft peaks form; gradually add sugar, beating until dissolved between additions.

preparation time 20 minutes
cooking time 1 hour (plus cooling time)
makes 16

cranberry and pistachio muesli slice

125g butter, chopped coarsely
⅓ cup (75g) firmly packed brown sugar
2 tablespoons honey
1½ cups (135g) rolled oats
½ cup (75g) self-raising flour
1 cup (130g) dried cranberries
1 cup (140g) roasted pistachios, chopped coarsely

1 Preheat oven to 180°C/160°C fan-assisted. Grease 20cm x 30cm shallow baking tin; line base with baking parchment, extending paper 5cm over long sides.
2 Stir butter, sugar and honey in medium saucepan over medium heat without boiling until sugar is dissolved. Stir in remaining ingredients. Press mixture firmly into tin.
3 Bake slice about 20 minutes. Cool in pan before cutting.

preparation time 20 minutes
cooking time 20 minutes (plus cooling time)
makes 30

pepita and sesame slice

90g butter, softened
1 teaspoon grated lemon rind
2 tablespoons caster sugar
1 egg
⅔ cup (100g) white plain flour
½ cup (80g) wholemeal plain flour
½ cup (80g) unsalted pepitas, chopped coarsely
¼ cup (80g) apricot jam
2 tablespoons sesame seeds, toasted

tip
This slice can be stored in an airtight container for up to 1 week.

1 Preheat oven to 200°C/180°C fan-assisted. Grease 23cm-square shallow cake tin; line base with baking parchment, extending paper 5cm over two opposite sides.
2 Beat butter, rind, sugar and egg in small bowl with electric mixer until light and fluffy. Stir in sifted flours and pepitas. Press mixture evenly into tin. Spread slice with jam; sprinkle with seeds.
3 Bake slice about 20 minutes or until browned lightly. Cool in tin before cutting.

preparation time 20 minutes
cooking time 20 minutes (plus cooling time)
makes 16

apple date squares

1¼ cups (185g) white plain flour
1¼ cups (200g) wholemeal plain flour
200g butter, chopped
½ cup (110g) caster sugar
1 egg, beaten lightly
1 tablespoon water, approximately
1 tablespoon milk
1 tablespoon raw sugar
2 teaspoons caster sugar, extra
apple date filling
1 medium apple (150g), peeled, sliced finely
1½ cups (225g) pitted dried dates, chopped coarsely
½ cup (125ml) water

1 Make apple date filling.
2 Preheat oven to 200°C/180°C fan-assisted. Grease 25cm x 30cm swiss roll tin; line base with baking parchment, extending paper 5cm over long sides.
3 Sift flours into large bowl, return husks from wholemeal flour to bowl; rub in butter with fingertips, stir in caster sugar. Add egg and enough water to mix to a firm dough. Knead on floured surface until smooth, cover; refrigerate 30 minutes.
4 Roll out half of the dough until large enough to cover base of tin; spread with cold apple date filling. Roll out remaining dough until large enough to cover filling; brush with milk, sprinkle with raw sugar.
5 Bake slice about 25 minutes. Cool in tin before cutting. Sprinkle with extra caster sugar.
apple date filling Place ingredients in small saucepan; simmer, covered, about 5 minutes or until pulpy. Blend or process mixture until smooth; cool.

preparation time 30 minutes (plus refrigeration time)
cooking time 30 minutes (plus cooling time)
makes 16

tip
This slice can be stored in an airtight container for up to 1 week.

marmalade almond squares

125g butter, softened, chopped
1 teaspoon almond essence
¼ cup (55g) caster sugar
1 cup (150g) plain flour
¼ cup (20g) desiccated coconut
⅓ cup (15g) flaked coconut
¼ cup (85g) marmalade, warmed
topping
90g butter, softened, chopped
2 teaspoons grated orange rind
⅓ cup (75g) caster sugar
2 eggs
1 cup (90g) desiccated coconut
1 cup (125g) ground almonds

1 Preheat oven to 200°C/180°C fan-assisted. Grease
19cm x 29cm baking tin; line base with baking parchment,
extending paper 5cm over long sides.
2 Beat butter, essence and sugar in small bowl with
electric mixer until smooth; stir in flour and desiccated
coconut. Press mixture into tin.
3 Bake slice about 15 minutes or until browned lightly.
4 Meanwhile, make topping.
5 Reduce oven to 180°C/160°C fan-assisted.
6 Spread hot slice with topping; sprinkle with flaked
coconut.
7 Bake about 20 minutes or until firm. Brush hot slice
with marmalade; cool in tin before slicing.
topping Beat butter, rind and sugar in small bowl with
electric mixer until smooth; add eggs, beat until combined
(mixture will look curdled at this stage). Stir in coconut and
ground almonds.

preparation time 30 minutes
cooking time 35 minutes (plus cooling time)
makes 18

tip
This slice can be
stored, covered, in
refrigerator for up
to 1 week.

nanaimo bars

185g butter, chopped
100g dark eating chocolate, chopped coarsely
1 egg
2 cups (200g) wheatmeal biscuit crumbs
1 cup (80g) desiccated coconut
⅔ cup (80g) finely chopped pecans
filling
60g butter, softened
1 teaspoon vanilla extract
2 cups (320g) icing sugar
2 tablespoons custard powder
¼ cup (60ml) milk
topping
30g dark eating chocolate
15g butter

1 Grease 19cm x 29cm baking tin; line base with baking parchment, extending paper 5cm over long sides.
2 Make filling.
3 Melt butter and chocolate in medium saucepan over low heat; remove from heat, stir in egg. Stir in biscuit crumbs, coconut and nuts. Press mixture firmly over base of tin. Spread evenly with filling.
4 Refrigerate slice until firm.
5 Make topping.
6 Drizzle slice with topping; refrigerate 3 hours or overnight until set. Cut into pieces before serving.
filling Beat butter and extract in small bowl with electric mixer until as white as possible; gradually beat in sifted icing sugar and custard powder, then milk.
topping Melt chocolate and butter in small heatproof bowl over hot water.

preparation time 45 minutes (plus refrigeration time)
makes 16

tip
This slice can be stored, covered, in the refrigerator for up to 2 weeks.

chocolate fudge brownies

150g butter, chopped
300g dark eating chocolate, chopped
1½ cups (330g) firmly packed brown sugar
3 eggs
1 teaspoon vanilla extract
¾ cup (110g) plain flour
¾ cup (140g) dark chocolate chips
½ cup (120g) soured cream
¾ cup (110g) roasted macadamias, chopped coarsely

1 Preheat oven to 180°C/160°C fan-assisted. Grease 19cm x 29cm baking tin; line base with baking parchment, extending paper 5cm over long sides.
2 Stir butter and dark chocolate in medium saucepan over low heat until smooth. Cool 10 minutes.
3 Stir sugar, eggs and extract into chocolate mixture, then sifted flour, chocolate chips, soured cream and nuts. Spread mixture into tin.
4 Bake brownies 40 minutes. Cover pan with foil; bake further 20 minutes. Cool in tin before cutting. Dust with sifted cocoa powder, if you like.

preparation time 20 minutes
cooking time 1 hour 5 minutes (plus cooling time)
makes 20

tips
You will need approximately 3 passionfruit for this recipe. This slice can be stored, refrigerated, in an airtight container, for up to 3 days.

vanilla slice

2 sheets ready-rolled puff pastry
½ cup (110g) caster sugar
½ cup (75g) cornflour
¼ cup (30g) custard powder
2½ cups (625ml) milk
30g butter
1 egg yolk
1 teaspoon vanilla extract
¾ cup (180ml) whipping cream
passionfruit icing
1½ cups (240g) icing sugar
1 teaspoon soft butter
¼ cup (60ml) passionfruit pulp

1   Preheat oven to 240°C/220°C fan-assisted. Grease deep 23cm-square cake tin; line base with foil, extending foil 10cm over two opposite sides.
2   Place each pastry sheet on a separate greased oven tray; bake about 15 minutes, cool. Flatten pastry with hand; place one pastry sheet in cake tin, trim to fit if necessary.
3   Meanwhile, combine sugar, cornflour and custard powder in medium saucepan; gradually add milk, stirring until smooth. Add butter; stir over heat until mixture boils and thickens. Simmer, stirring, 3 minutes or until custard is thick and smooth. Remove from heat; stir in egg yolk and extract. Cover surface of custard with cling film; cool to room temperature.
4   Make passionfruit icing.
5   Whip cream until firm peaks form. Fold cream into custard, in two batches. Spread custard mixture over pastry in tin. Top with remaining pastry, trim to fit if necessary; press down slightly. Spread pastry with icing; refrigerate 3 hours or overnight.
passionfruit icing Place sifted icing sugar, butter and pulp in small heatproof bowl over small saucepan of simmering water; stir until icing is spreadable.

preparation time 20 minutes (plus cooling and refrigeration time)
cooking time 35 minutes
makes 16

apricot choc-chip muesli bars

125g butter, chopped
½ cup (110g) firmly packed brown sugar
1 tablespoon honey
2¼ cups (200g) rolled oats
¼ cup (40g) sunflower kernels
¼ cup (20g) desiccated coconut
½ teaspoon ground cinnamon
½ cup (75g) chopped dried apricots
2 tablespoons dark chocolate chips

1 Preheat oven to 160°C/140°C fan-assisted. Grease 20cm x 30cm shallow baking tin; line base with baking parchment, extending paper 5cm over long sides.
2 Stir butter, sugar and honey in medium saucepan over low heat until sugar is dissolved. Transfer mixture to medium bowl; stir in oats, sunflower kernels, coconut, cinnamon and apricots. Press mixture into tin; sprinkle with chocolate chips.
3 Bake muesli bars about 30 minutes or until browned lightly. Cut into pieces while still warm; cool in tin.

preparation time 15 minutes
cooking time 30 minutes (plus cooling time)
makes 8

tip
Both these slices can be stored in an airtight container for up to 1 week.

raspberry coconut slice

90g butter, softened
½ cup (110g) caster sugar
1 egg
¼ cup (35g) self-raising flour
⅔ cup (100g) plain flour
1 tablespoon custard powder
⅔ cup (220g) raspberry jam
coconut topping
2 cups (160g) desiccated coconut
¼ cup (55g) caster sugar
2 eggs, beaten lightly

1 Preheat oven to 180°C/160°C fan-assisted. Grease 20cm x 30cm shallow baking tin; line base with baking parchment, extending paper 5cm over long sides.
2 Beat butter, sugar and egg in small bowl with electric mixer until light and fluffy. Transfer to medium bowl; stir in sifted flours and custard powder. Spread dough onto base of tin; spread with jam.
3 Make coconut topping; sprinkle topping over jam.
4 Bake slice about 40 minutes. Cool in tin before slicing.
coconut topping Combine ingredients in small bowl.

preparation time 25 minutes (plus cooling time)
cooking time 40 minutes
makes 20

chocolate and peanut butter swirl

360g white eating chocolate,
chopped coarsely
½ cup (140g) smooth peanut butter
400g dark eating chocolate,
chopped coarsely

1 Grease 20cm x 30cm shallow baking tin; line base
with baking parchment, extending paper 5cm above
long sides.
2 Stir white chocolate in small heatproof bowl over
small saucepan of simmering water until smooth; cool
5 minutes. Add peanut butter; stir until smooth.
3 Stir dark chocolate in small heatproof bowl over
small saucepan of simmering water until smooth;
cool slightly.
4 Drop alternate spoonfuls of white chocolate mixture
and dark chocolate into tin. Gently shake tin to level
mixture; pull a skewer backwards and forwards through
mixtures several times for a marbled effect.
5 Stand slice at room temperature about 2 hours or until
set. Cut into small pieces.

preparation time 15 minutes
cooking time 10 minutes
makes about 72

chewy chocolate slice

tip
This slice can be stored in an airtight container for up to 1 week.

125g butter, melted
1 cup (220g) firmly packed brown sugar
1 egg, beaten lightly
1 teaspoon vanilla extract
½ cup (75g) plain flour
¼ cup (35g) self-raising flour
2 tablespoons cocoa powder
½ cup (45g) desiccated coconut
1 tablespoon desiccated coconut, extra
chocolate icing
1 cup (160g) icing sugar
2 tablespoons cocoa powder
10g butter, melted
1½ tablespoons hot water, approximately

1 Preheat oven to 180°C/160°C fan-assisted. Grease 19cm x 29cm baking tin; line base with baking parchment, extending paper 5cm over long sides.
2 Combine butter, sugar, egg and extract in medium bowl. Stir in sifted flours and cocoa powder, then coconut. Spread mixture over base of tin.
3 Bake slice about 30 minutes or until firm.
4 Meanwhile, make chocolate icing.
5 Spread hot slice with chocolate icing; sprinkle with extra coconut. Cool in tin before cutting.
chocolate icing Sift icing sugar and cocoa powder into medium bowl, stir in combined butter and water until spreadable.

preparation time 20 minutes
cooking time 30 minutes (plus cooling time)
makes 12

apple and prune slice

4 medium apples (600g)
¾ cup (135g) coarsely chopped pitted prunes
2½ cups (625ml) water
½ teaspoon ground cinnamon
½ teaspoon ground nutmeg
2 tablespoons ground hazelnuts
2 sheets ready-rolled shortcrust pastry
1 tablespoon caster sugar

1 Peel and core apples; slice thinly. Place apples, prunes and the water in medium saucepan; bring to the boil. Reduce heat; simmer, covered, 10 minutes or until apples are just tender. Drain well; cool 15 minutes.
2 Combine spices and ground hazelnuts in medium bowl; gently stir in apple mixture.

3 Preheat oven to 200°C/180°C fan-assisted. Grease 20cm x 30cm shallow baking tin; line base with baking parchment.
4 Roll one pastry sheet large enough to cover base of tin; place in tin, trim edges. Cover pastry with baking parchment, fill with dried beans or rice; bake 15 minutes. Remove paper and beans; bake further 5 minutes. Spread apple mixture over pastry.
5 Roll remaining pastry sheet large enough to fit tin; place over apple filling. Brush pastry with a little water, sprinkle with sugar; score pastry in crosshatch pattern.
6 Bake slice about 45 minutes. Cool in tin before slicing.

preparation time 20 minutes
cooking time 1 hour 10 minutes (plus cooling time)
makes 24

chocolate macadamia slice

tip
Macadamias can be replaced with any other variety of nut.

200g butter, chopped
⅓ cup (115g) golden syrup
⅓ cup (35g) drinking chocolate
¼ cup (25g) cocoa powder
500g plain sweet biscuits, chopped finely
½ cup (75g) toasted macadamias, chopped coarsely
200g dark eating chocolate

1 Line 20cm x 30cm baking tin with cling film.
2 Combine butter, syrup, drinking chocolate and sifted cocoa in medium saucepan; stir over medium heat until mixture is smooth. Add biscuits and nuts; stir to combine.
3 Press mixture into prepared tin, cover; refrigerate until firm.
4 Stir chocolate in medium heatproof bowl over simmering water until smooth. Spread chocolate over slice; refrigerate, uncovered, until firm. Cut into pieces to serve.

preparation time 15 minutes (plus refrigeration time)
cooking time 5 minutes
makes 30

chocolate rum and raisin slice

125g butter, chopped coarsely
200g dark eating chocolate, chopped coarsely
½ cup (110g) caster sugar
1 cup (170g) coarsely chopped raisins
2 eggs, beaten lightly
1½ cups (225g) plain flour
1 tablespoon dark rum

1 Preheat oven to 160°C/140°C fan-assisted. Grease 20cm x 30cm shallow baking tin.
2 Stir butter, chocolate, sugar and raisins in medium saucepan over low heat until chocolate is melted. Cool to room temperature.
3 Stir remaining ingredients into chocolate mixture. Spread into tin. Bake slice about 30 minutes. Cool in tin before cutting.

preparation time 20 minutes
cooking time 35 minutes
makes 32

tip
Rum has a very distinctive taste, we like to use an underproof rum, but can use the stronger overproof variety, if you like.

white chocolate, nut and berry blondies

125g butter, chopped coarsely
300g white eating chocolate, chopped coarsely
¾ cup (165g) caster sugar
2 eggs
¾ cup (110g) plain flour
½ cup (75g) self-raising flour
½ cup (75g) coarsely chopped roasted macadamias
150g fresh or frozen raspberries

1   Preheat oven to 180°C/160°C fan-assisted. Grease 23cm-square baking tin; line base with baking parchment, extending paper 5cm over two opposite sides.
2   Stir butter and two-thirds of the chocolate in medium saucepan over low heat until smooth. Cool 10 minutes.
3   Stir sugar and eggs into chocolate mixture, then sifted flours, remaining chocolate, nuts and berries. Spread mixture into tin.
4   Bake blondies about 40 minutes. Cool in tin before cutting. Dust with sifted icing sugar, if you like.

preparation time 20 minutes
cooking time 45 minutes (plus cooling time)
makes 25

caramel and chocolate slice

½ cup (75g) plain flour
½ cup (75g) self-raising flour
1 cup (90g) rolled oats
¾ cup (165g) firmly packed brown sugar
150g butter, melted
125g dark eating chocolate, chopped coarsely
½ cup (55g) coarsely chopped walnuts
¼ cup (35g) plain flour, extra
½ cup (125ml) Dulce de leche (caramel topping)

1 Preheat oven to 180°C/160°C fan-assisted. Grease 19cm x 29cm baking tin; line base with baking parchment, extending paper 5cm over long sides.
2 Combine flours, oats and sugar in medium bowl; stir in butter. Press half the mixture into base of tin.
3 Bake 10 minutes. Remove from oven; sprinkle with chocolate and nuts.
4 Blend extra flour and caramel topping in small bowl; drizzle evenly over chocolate and nuts. Sprinkle with remaining oat mixture.
5 Bake further 15 minutes. Cool in tin before cutting.

preparation time 20 minutes
cooking time 25 minutes (plus cooling time)
makes 15

dutch ginger and almond slice

1¾ cups (255g) plain flour
1 cup (220g) caster sugar
⅔ cup (150g) coarsely chopped glacé ginger
½ cup (80g) blanched almonds, chopped coarsely
1 egg
185g butter, melted
2 teaspoons icing sugar

1   Preheat oven to 180°C/160°C fan-assisted. Grease
20cm x 30cm shallow baking tin; line base with baking
parchment, extending paper 5cm over long sides.
2   Combine sifted flour, sugar, ginger, nuts and egg in
medium bowl; stir in butter. Press mixture into tin.
3   Bake slice about 35 minutes. Stand slice in tin
10 minutes; transfer to wire rack to cool. Cut into squares;
dust with sifted icing sugar.

preparation time 15 minutes
cooking time 35 minutes (plus standing time)
makes 20

tip
Stem ginger can be
substituted for glacé
ginger if rinsed with
warm water and dried
before use.

chocolate caramel slice

½ cup (75g) plain flour
½ cup (75g) self-raising flour
1 cup (80g) desiccated coconut
1 cup (220g) firmly packed brown sugar
125g butter, melted
caramel filling
395g can sweetened condensed milk
30g butter
2 tablespoons golden syrup
chocolate topping
200g dark eating chocolate, chopped coarsely
2 teaspoons vegetable oil

1 Preheat oven to 180°C/160°C fan-assisted. Grease 20cm x 30cm shallow baking tin; line base with baking parchment, extending paper 5cm over long sides.
2 Combine sifted flours, coconut, sugar and butter in medium bowl; press mixture evenly over base of tin. Bake about 15 minutes or until browned lightly.
3 Meanwhile, make caramel filling.
4 Pour filling over base; bake 10 minutes. Cool.
5 Meanwhile, make chocolate topping.
6 Pour warm topping over caramel. Refrigerate 3 hours or overnight.
caramel filling Stir ingredients in small saucepan over medium heat about 15 minutes or until golden brown.
chocolate topping Stir ingredients in small heatproof bowl over small saucepan of simmering water until chocolate melts and is smooth.

VARIATIONS
mocha filling Dissolve 2 teaspoons instant coffee granules in 1 tablespoon hot water; add to the condensed milk mixture with 2 tablespoons coffee-flavoured liqueur. Cook as in step 4.
white chocolate topping Replace dark eating chocolate with 180g white eating chocolate.

preparation time 20 minutes
cooking time 25 minutes (plus refrigeration time)
makes 16

tip
This slice can be stored, in an airtight container, in the refrigerator for up to 4 days.

hazelnut brownies

125g butter
200g dark eating chocolate, chopped coarsely
½ cup (110g) caster sugar
2 eggs, beaten lightly
1¼ cups (185g) plain flour
½ cup (70g) roasted hazelnuts, chopped coarsely
1 cup (190g) white chocolate chips

1 Preheat oven to 180°C/160°C fan-assisted. Grease deep 19cm-square cake tin; line base with baking parchment, extending paper 5cm above two opposite sides.
2 Stir butter and chocolate in medium saucepan over low heat until smooth. Stir in sugar; cook, stirring, 5 minutes. Cool 10 minutes.
3 Stir in egg and sifted flour, then nuts and chocolate chips. Spread mixture into tin.
4 Bake brownies about 30 minutes. Cool in tin before cutting. Dust with icing sugar, if you like.

preparation time 15 minutes
cooking time 25 minutes
makes 12

no-bake chocolate slice

200g packet white marshmallows
1 tablespoon water
90g butter, chopped
200g dark eating chocolate, chopped coarsely
125g digestive biscuits, chopped coarsely
½ cup (125g) halved glacé cherries
½ cup (75g) roasted hazelnuts
½ cup (50g) walnuts
200g dark eating chocolate, melted, extra
60g butter, melted, extra

1 Grease two 8cm x 25cm bar cake tins; line bases with baking parchment, extending 5cm above long sides.
2 Stir marshmallows, the water and butter in medium saucepan constantly over low heat until marshmallows are melted. Remove saucepan from heat; stir in chocolate until melted.
3 Add biscuits, cherries and nuts to marshmallow mixture; stir gently until ingredients are combined. Spread mixture evenly between tins (do not crush biscuits). Cover; refrigerate 1 hour.
4 Combine extra chocolate and extra butter; spread mixture evenly over slices. Refrigerate 1 hour or until firm. Remove slices from tins. Peel away paper; cut each into 12 slices.

preparation time 20 minutes (plus refrigeration time)
cooking time 5 minutes
makes 24

tips
This slice can be stored, covered, in the refrigerator for up to 1 week. Pecans can be used instead of walnuts, if you like.

fruity white chocolate bars

⅔ cup (90g) slivered almonds
1¼ cups (210g) brazil nuts, chopped coarsely
1½ cups (135g) desiccated coconut
1 cup (150g) chopped dried apricots
1 cup (150g) currants
¼ cup (35g) plain flour
250g white eating chocolate, melted
½ cup (160g) apricot jam, warmed
½ cup (180g) honey

1 Preheat oven to 160°C/140°C fan-assisted. Grease 19cm x 29cm baking tin; line base with baking parchment, extending paper 5cm over long sides.
2 Combine nuts, coconut, fruit and flour in large bowl. Stir in combined hot melted chocolate, sieved jam and honey. Spread mixture into tin.
3 Bake slice about 45 minutes. Cool in tin before cutting.

preparation time 15 minutes
cooking time 45 minutes (plus cooling time)
makes 24

tip
This slice can be stored, covered, in the refrigerator for up to 1 week.

cashew ginger squares

125g butter, softened
¼ cup (55g) caster sugar
1 cup (150g) self-raising flour
1 teaspoon ground ginger
topping
½ cup (80g) icing sugar
60g butter
2 tablespoons golden syrup
1 cup (150g) unsalted roasted cashews,
chopped coarsely
¼ cup (50g) finely chopped stem ginger

1   Preheat oven to 180°C/160°C fan-assisted. Grease
20cm x 30cm shallow baking tin; line base with baking
parchment, extending paper 5cm over long sides.
2   Beat butter and sugar in small bowl with electric mixer
until light and fluffy; stir in sifted flour and ginger. Spread
mixture over base of tin.
3   Bake base about 20 minutes or until browned lightly;
cool in tin.
4   Meanwhile, make topping; spread hot topping over
cold base. Cool.
topping   Stir sifted icing sugar, butter and syrup in small
saucepan over heat until butter is melted. Stir in nuts
and ginger.

preparation time 20 minutes
cooking time 20 minutes
makes 30

tip
This slice can be
stored, covered, in
the refrigerator for
up to 1 week.

hazelnut caramel slice

200g butter, chopped
½ cup (50g) cocoa powder
2 cups (440g) firmly packed brown sugar
1 teaspoon vanilla extract
2 eggs, beaten lightly
1½ cups (225g) plain flour
200g dark eating chocolate, melted, cooled
1 tablespoon vegetable oil
caramel filling
185g butter, chopped
½ cup (110g) caster sugar
2 tablespoons golden syrup
¾ cup (180ml) sweetened condensed milk
1¼ cups (175g) roasted hazelnuts

1 Preheat oven to 170°C/150°C fan-assisted. Grease 20cm x 30cm shallow baking tin; line base and two long sides with baking parchment.
2 Stir butter with sifted cocoa in medium saucepan over low heat until smooth. Add sugar; stir until dissolved. Remove from heat; add vanilla extract, egg and sifted flour, mix well. Spread mixture into tin; bake, uncovered, 20 minutes; cool 10 minutes.
3 Meanwhile, make caramel filling.
4 Spread caramel filling evenly over base; refrigerate at least 30 minutes or until firm. Combine chocolate and oil in small bowl, spread over caramel filling; refrigerate until set.
caramel filling Stir butter, sugar, syrup and condensed milk in medium saucepan over low heat until butter is melted. Increase heat to medium; simmer, stirring, 10 minutes or until mixture is a dark caramel colour. Remove from heat; stir in nuts.

preparation time 20 minutes (plus refrigeration time)
cooking time 30 minutes
makes 20

hedgehog slice

¾ cup (180ml) sweetened condensed milk
60g butter
125g dark eating chocolate, chopped coarsely
150g plain sweet biscuits, broken into small pieces
⅓ cup (45g) unsalted roasted peanuts
⅓ cup (55g) sultanas

preparation time 10 minutes
(plus refrigeration time)
cooking time 5 minutes
makes 12

1   Grease 8cm x 26cm bar cake tin; line base with baking parchment, extending paper 5cm over long sides.
2   Stir condensed milk and butter in small saucepan over low heat until smooth. Remove from heat; stir in chocolate until smooth.
3   Place biscuit pieces in large bowl with nuts and sultanas. Add chocolate mixture; stir to combine.
4   Spread mixture into tin. Cover; refrigerate about 4 hours or until firm. Remove from tin; cut into slices.

tip
This slice can be stored in an airtight container for up to 1 week.

coconut yogurt slice

tip
This slice can be stored in an airtight container for up to 1 week.

125g butter, softened
1 cup (220g) caster sugar
2 eggs
½ cup (40g) desiccated coconut
1 cup (150g) self-raising flour
½ cup (75g) plain flour
200g greek-style natural yogurt
⅔ cup (160ml) milk
coconut frosting
2 cups (320g) icing sugar
1⅓ cups (100g) desiccated coconut
2 egg whites, beaten lightly
pink food colouring

1 Preheat oven to 180°C/160°C fan-assisted. Grease deep 23cm-square cake tin; line base with baking parchment.
2 Beat butter and sugar in small bowl with electric mixer until light and fluffy. Beat in eggs, one at a time. Transfer mixture to large bowl; stir in coconut, sifted flours, yogurt and milk, in two batches. Spread mixture into tin.
3 Bake about 40 minutes. Stand slice in tin 5 minutes; turn, top-side up, onto wire rack to cool.
4 Meanwhile, make coconut frosting. Drop alternate spoonfuls of white and pink frosting onto slice; marble over top of slice before slicing.
coconut frosting Sift icing sugar into medium bowl; stir in coconut and egg white. Place half the mixture in small bowl; tint with pink colouring.

preparation time 25 minutes
cooking time 40 minutes
makes 12

rosewater baklava

1 cup (160g) blanched almonds
1 cup (140g) shelled pistachios
2 teaspoons ground cinnamon
1 teaspoon ground cloves
1 teaspoon ground nutmeg
18 sheets filo pastry
80g butter, melted
rosewater syrup
1 cup (250ml) water
1 cup (220g) caster sugar
¼ cup (90g) honey
1 teaspoon rosewater

1 Preheat oven to 180°C/160°C fan-assisted. Grease deep 23cm-square cake tin.
2 Process nuts and spices until chopped finely; spread nut mixture onto oven tray. Roast, uncovered, about 10 minutes or until browned lightly.
3 Increase oven temperature to 200°C/180°C fan-assisted.
4 Cut pastry sheets to fit base of tin; layer three pastry squares, brushing each with butter; place in tin, sprinkle with ⅓ cup of the nut mixture. Repeat layering with remaining pastry, butter and nut mixture, ending with a layer of pastry.
5 Using sharp knife, cut baklava into quarters; cut each quarter in half on the diagonal, then cut each triangle in half. Bake 25 minutes.
6 Reduce oven temperature to 150°C/130°C fan-assisted, bake baklava further 10 minutes.
7 Meanwhile, make rosewater syrup.
8 Pour hot syrup over hot baklava; cool in tin.
rosewater syrup Combine ingredients in small saucepan. Stir over heat, without boiling, until sugar dissolves; bring to a boil then simmer, uncovered, without stirring, about 5 minutes or until thickened slightly.

preparation time 15 minutes
cooking time 35 minutes
makes 16

triple choc brownies

125g butter, chopped coarsely
200g dark eating chocolate, chopped coarsely
½ cup (110g) caster sugar
2 eggs
1¼ cups (185g) plain flour
150g white eating chocolate, chopped coarsely
100g milk eating chocolate, chopped coarsely

1 Preheat oven to 180°C/160°C fan-assisted. Grease deep 19cm-square cake tin; line base with baking parchment, extending paper 5cm over two opposite sides.
2 Stir butter and dark chocolate in medium saucepan over low heat until smooth. Cool 10 minutes.
3 Stir sugar and eggs into chocolate mixture, then sifted flour and white and milk chocolates. Spread mixture in tin.
4 Bake about 35 minutes. Cool in tin before cutting.

preparation time 20 minutes
cooking time 40 minutes (plus cooling time)
makes 16

glace fruit slice with limoncello cream

90g butter, softened
1 tablespoon finely grated lemon rind
¾ cup (165g) caster sugar
2 eggs
¾ cup (110g) plain flour
½ cup (75g) self-raising flour
⅓ cup (80ml) milk
⅔ cup (150g) coarsely chopped glacé pineapple
⅔ cup (170g) coarsely chopped glacé apricots
⅔ cup (170g) coarsely chopped glacé peaches
¾ cup (110g) coarsely chopped dried pears
¾ cup (110g) toasted shelled pistachios
lemon syrup
½ cup (125ml) lemon juice
1 cup (220g) caster sugar
limoncello cream
300ml whipping cream
2 tablespoons limoncello

1 Preheat oven to 170°C/150°C fan-assisted. Line 20cm x 30cm shallow baking tin with baking parchment, extending paper 3cm over long sides.
2 Beat butter, rind and sugar in small bowl with electric mixer until light and fluffy. Add eggs, one at a time, beating well between additions. Mixture may curdle at this stage, but will come together later.
3 Transfer mixture to large bowl; stir in sifted flours, milk, fruit and nuts. Spread mixture into prepared tin. Bake, uncovered, about 45 minutes.
4 Meanwhile, make lemon syrup.
5 Remove slice from oven; pour hot syrup over hot slice in tin. Cover; refrigerate overnight.
6 Make limoncello cream.
7 Cut slice into small squares; serve with the limoncello cream.

lemon syrup Stir ingredients in small saucepan over heat, without boiling, until sugar dissolves; bring to a boil. Reduce heat; simmer, uncovered, without stirring, about 10 minutes or until thickened slightly.

limoncello cream Beat ingredients in small bowl with electric mixer until soft peaks form.

preparation time 30 minutes
cooking time 45 minutes (plus refrigeration time)
makes 24

tips
You can substitute the limoncello with any lemon-flavoured liqueur or with an orange-flavoured one such as Cointreau. You will need approximately five lemons for this recipe.

flourless hazelnut chocolate slice

⅓ cup (35g) cocoa powder
⅓ cup (80ml) hot water
150g dark eating chocolate, melted
150g butter, melted
1⅓ cups (275g) firmly packed brown sugar
1 cup (100g) ground hazelnuts
4 eggs, separated
1 tablespoon cocoa powder, extra

1 Preheat oven to 180°C/160°C fan-assisted. Grease deep 19cm-square cake tin; line base and sides with baking parchment.
2 Blend cocoa with the hot water in large bowl until smooth. Stir in chocolate, butter, sugar, ground hazelnuts and egg yolks.
3 Beat egg whites in small bowl with electric mixer until soft peaks form; fold into chocolate mixture in two batches. Pour mixture into tin.
4 Bake about 1 hour or until firm. Stand slice in tin 15 minutes; turn, top-side up, onto wire rack to cool. Dust with sifted extra cocoa.

preparation time 20 minutes (plus standing time)
cooking time 1 hour
serves 9

cherry almond slice

4 egg whites
100g butter, melted
1 tablespoon milk
½ teaspoon vanilla extract
1 cup (125g) ground almonds
1 cup (160g) icing sugar
⅓ cup (50g) self-raising flour
1 vanilla pod
⅔ cup (100g) frozen cherries, chopped coarsely

1 Preheat oven to 170°C/150°C fan-assisted. Grease 19cm x 29cm baking tin; line base and two long sides with baking parchment, extending paper 5cm over long sides.
2 Place egg whites in large bowl, whisk with fork until combined. Add butter, milk, extract, ground almonds and sifted icing sugar and flour; stir until just combined. Split vanilla pod in half lengthways; scrape seeds from pod, stir seeds into mixture.
3 Pour mixture into tin; sprinkle cherries over mixture. Bake about 30 minutes; stand in tin 10 minutes before lifting slice onto wire rack to cool. Dust with sifted icing sugar, if desired.

preparation time 15 minutes
baking time 40 minutes
makes 16

tips
This slice can be made up to 4 days ahead and refrigerated, covered. It can also be frozen for up to 3 months. Ground hazelnuts are a flour-like substance made after the nuts have been roasted.

dark chocolate mud slice

250g butter, chopped
2 cups (440g) caster sugar
½ cup (125ml) milk
½ cup (125ml) strong black coffee
½ cup (125ml) bourbon
1 teaspoon vanilla extract
200g dark eating chocolate, chopped coarsely
1½ cups (225g) plain flour
¼ cup (35g) self-raising flour
¼ cup (25g) cocoa powder
2 eggs
chocolate ganache
½ cup (125ml) double cream
200g dark eating chocolate, chopped coarsely

1 Preheat oven to 160°C/140°C fan-assisted. Grease deep 23cm-square cake tin; line base with baking parchment.
2 Stir butter, sugar, milk, coffee, bourbon, extract and chocolate in medium saucepan over low heat until smooth. Transfer to large bowl; cool 15 minutes. Whisk in sifted flours and cocoa then eggs. Pour mixture into tin.
3 Bake about 1½ hours. Stand slice in tin 5 minutes; turn, top-side up, onto wire rack to cool.
4 Meanwhile, make chocolate ganache.
5 Spread cold cake with chocolate ganache.
chocolate ganache Bring cream to the boil in small saucepan. Remove from heat, add chocolate; stir until smooth. Stand 10 minutes before using.

preparation time 25 minutes (plus cooling time)
cooking time 1 hour 40 minutes
serves 12

snickers rocky road

4 x 60g Snickers™ bars, chopped coarsely
1 cup (35g) Rice Krispies™
150g toasted marshmallows, chopped coarsely
1 cup (150g) toasted unsalted peanuts
400g milk eating chocolate, chopped coarsely
2 teaspoons vegetable oil

1 Grease 19cm x 29cm baking tin. Line base and two long sides with baking parchment, extending paper 2cm above sides of tin.
2 Combine Snickers™, Rice Krispies™, marshmallows and nuts in large bowl. Stir chocolate and oil in small saucepan over low heat until smooth. Cool 5 minutes.
3 Pour chocolate mixture into Snickers™ mixture; mix until well combined. Spoon rocky road mixture into prepared tin; refrigerate, covered, about 30 minutes or until set. Remove from tin, trim edges of mixture; cut into 3cm squares. Store, covered, in the refrigerator.

preparation time 15 minutes (plus refrigeration time)
cooking time 5 minutes
makes 54 squares

nutty choc-orange slice

1½ cups (240g) blanched almonds
2½ cups (250g) walnuts
200g dark eating chocolate, chopped coarsely
250g butter, softened
1 teaspoon vanilla extract
1 cup (220g) caster sugar
5 eggs, separated
1 tablespoon finely grated orange rind
1 tablespoon icing sugar

1   Preheat oven to 150°C/130°C fan-assisted. Grease 23cm-square cake tin; line base and sides with baking parchment.
2   Blend or process nuts and chocolate until chopped finely.
3   Beat butter, extract and sugar in small bowl with electric mixer until light and fluffy. Beat in egg yolks, one at a time. Transfer mixture to large bowl; stir in chocolate mixture and rind.
4   Beat egg whites in small bowl with electric mixer until soft peaks form; fold into chocolate mixture, in two batches. Pour mixture into tin.
5   Bake about 1¼ hours. Cool in tin. Cover; refrigerate 3 hours or overnight.
6   Cut into squares; serve squares dusted with sifted icing sugar.

preparation time 30 minutes
(plus cooling and refrigeration time)
cooking time 1 hour 15 minutes
serves 16

chocolate panforte

2 sheets rice paper
¾ cup (110g) plain flour
2 tablespoons cocoa powder
½ teaspoon ground cinnamon
½ teaspoon ground ginger
½ cup (150g) coarsely chopped glacé figs
½ cup (85g) dried dates, pitted, halved
½ cup (125g) coarsely chopped glacé peaches
¼ cup (50g) red glacé cherries, halved
¼ cup (50g) green glacé cherries, halved
½ cup (80g) toasted blanched almonds
½ cup (75g) toasted unsalted cashews
½ cup (75g) toasted hazelnuts
½ cup (75g) toasted macadamia nuts
⅓ cup (120g) honey
⅓ cup (75g) caster sugar
⅓ cup (75g) firmly packed brown sugar
2 tablespoons water
100g dark eating chocolate, melted

1 Preheat oven to 170°C/150°C fan-assisted. Grease 20cm square cake tin; line base with rice paper sheets.
2 Sift flour, cocoa and spices into large bowl; stir in fruit and nuts.
3 Combine honey, sugars and the water in small saucepan; stir over heat, without boiling, until sugar dissolves. Simmer; uncovered, without stirring, 5 minutes. Pour hot syrup, then chocolate, into nut mixture; stir until well combined. Press mixture firmly into prepared tin.
4 Bake for about 45 minutes; cool in tin.
5 Remove panforte from tin; wrap in foil. Stand overnight; cut into thin slices to serve.

preparation time 25 minutes (plus standing time)
cooking time 55 minutes
makes 30

tips
Rice paper can be found in specialist food stores and some supermarkets.

peanut slices

60g butter
2 tablespoons caster sugar
1 egg, lightly beaten
1 cup (150g) plain flour
2 tablespoons self-raising flour
¼ cup raspberry jam
topping
2 eggs, separated
¾ cup (165g) caster sugar
30g butter, melted
1 cup (90g) desiccated coconut
1½ cups (250g) chopped roasted unsalted peanuts
1 cup (30g) cornflakes

1 Preheat oven to 200°C/180°C fan-assisted. Grease 20cm x 30cm shallow baking tin.
2 Beat butter and sugar in small bowl with electric mixer until creamy; gradually add egg, beat until combined. Stir in sifted flours.
3 Press mixture over base of prepared tin, prick well with fork. Bake for about 10 minutes or until base is firm; cool.
4 Meanwhile, make topping. Reduce oven temperature to 180°C/160°C fan-assisted.
5 Spread jam over cooled base, spread topping over jam. Bake for about 30 minutes or until browned and firm; cool in tin. Refrigerate 1 hour before cutting into slices .
topping Beat egg yolks, sugar and butter in small bowl until thick and creamy; stir in coconut and peanuts. Beat egg whites in small bowl until soft peaks form; fold into nut mixture with cornfakes.

preparation time 15 minutes
cooking time 40 minutes
makes about 15

lime and poppy seed syrup slice

¼ cup (40g) poppy seeds
½ cup (125ml) milk
250g butter, softened
1 tablespoon finely grated lime rind
1¼ cups (275g) caster sugar
4 eggs
2¼ cups (335g) self-raising flour
¾ cup (110g) plain flour
1 cup (240g) soured cream
lime syrup
½ cup (125ml) lime juice
1 cup (250ml) water
1 cup (220g) caster sugar

lime syrup Stir ingredients in small saucepan over heat, without boiling, until sugar dissolves. Simmer, uncovered, without stirring, 5 minutes.

1 Preheat oven to 180°C/160°C fan-assisted. Grease deep 23cm-square cake tin. Combine poppy seeds and milk in small jug; soak 10 minutes.
2 Beat butter, rind and sugar in small bowl with electric mixer until light and fluffy. Beat in eggs, one at a time. Transfer mixture to large bowl; stir in sifted flours, soured cream and poppy seed mixture, in two batches. Spread mixture into tin.
3 Bake about 1 hour. Stand slice in tin 5 minutes; turn, top-side up, onto wire rack over tray.
4 Meanwhile, make syrup; pour hot syrup over hot cake.

preparation time 20 minutes
cooking time 1 hour
serves 9

tips
You can substitute the same weight of other citrus fruit – lemons, mandarins, oranges, etc – for the limes if you like.

roulades

berry cream roulade

3 eggs
½ cup (110g) caster sugar
½ cup (75g) cornflour
1 tablespoon custard powder
1 teaspoon cream of tartar
½ teaspoon bicarbonate of soda
1 tablespoon caster sugar, extra
1 tablespoon icing sugar
berry cream
¾ cup (180ml) whipping cream
1 teaspoon vanilla extract
1 tablespoon icing sugar
1 cup (150g) frozen blackberries, chopped coarsely

1 Preheat oven to 180°C/ 160°C fan-assisted. Grease 25cm x 30cm swiss roll tin; line base and two long sides with baking parchment, extending paper 5cm over long sides.
2 Beat eggs and caster sugar in small bowl with electric mixer about 5 minutes or until sugar is dissolved and mixture is thick and creamy; transfer to large bowl.

3 Sift cornflour, custard powder, cream of tartar and soda together twice onto paper then sift over egg mixture; gently fold dry ingredients into egg mixture. Spread sponge mixture into tin; bake about 12 minutes.
4 Meanwhile, place a piece of baking parchment cut the same size as swiss roll tin on worktop; sprinkle evenly with extra caster sugar.
5 Turn sponge onto sugared paper; peel away lining paper. Use serrated knife to cut away crisp edges from all sides of sponge, cover sponge with a tea towel; cool.
6 Meanwhile, make berry cream; spread cream over sponge. Using paper as a guide, roll sponge gently from long side to enclose filling. Dust with sifted icing sugar.

berry cream Beat cream, extract and icing sugar in small bowl with electric mixer until soft peaks form; fold in thawed berries.

preparation time 15 minutes
cooking time 12 minutes
serves 10

ginger fluff roll

3 eggs
⅔ cup (150g) caster sugar
⅔ cup (100g) cornflour
1 teaspoon cream of tartar
½ teaspoon bicarbonate of soda
1 teaspoon cocoa powder
2 teaspoons ground ginger
½ teaspoon ground cinnamon
¾ cup (180ml) whipping cream
2 tablespoons golden syrup
1 teaspoon ground ginger, extra

1 Preheat oven to 180°C/160°C fan-assisted. Grease 25cm x 30cm swiss roll tin; line base with baking parchment, extending paper 5cm over long sides.
2 Beat eggs and ½ cup of the sugar in small bowl with electric mixer until thick and creamy and sugar is dissolved. Transfer mixture to large bowl; fold in triple-sifted dry ingredients. Spread mixture into tin.

3 Bake about 12 minutes.
4 Meanwhile, place piece of baking parchment cut the same size as tin on worktop; sprinkle with remaining sugar. Turn sponge onto paper; peel lining paper away. Cool; trim all sides of sponge.
5 Beat cream, syrup and extra ginger in small bowl with electric mixer until firm peaks form; spread over sponge. Using paper as a guide, roll sponge from long side. Cover with cling film; refrigerate 30 minutes.

preparation time 25 minutes (plus refrigeration time)
cooking time 12 minutes
serves 10

tips
Filled sponges and rolls are best eaten on the day they are made. Unfilled sponges can be frozen for up to 2 months.

sponge roll with jam and cream

3 eggs
⅔ cup (150g) caster sugar
½ cup (75g) cornflour
2 tablespoons custard powder
¾ teaspoon cream of tartar
½ teaspoon bicarbonate of soda
⅓ cup (110g) raspberry jam
¾ cup (180ml) whipping cream, whipped

1   Preheat oven to 180°C/160°C fan-assisted. Grease
25cm x 30cm swiss roll tin; line base with baking
parchment, extending paper 5cm over long sides.
2   Beat eggs and ½ cup of the caster sugar in small bowl
with electric mixer until thick, creamy and sugar has
dissolved. Fold in triple-sifted dry ingredients.
Spread mixture into tin.
3   Bake cake about 12 minutes.
4   Meanwhile, place piece of baking parchment cut the
same size as tin on worktop; sprinkle with remaining caster
sugar. Turn sponge onto paper; peel lining paper away.
Cool; trim all sides of sponge.
5   Spread sponge with jam then cream. Using paper as
a guide, roll sponge from short side. Cover with cling film;
refrigerate 30 minutes.

preparation time 25 minutes (plus refrigeration time)
cooking time 12 minutes
serves 10

tip
Filled sponges
and rolls are best
eaten on the day
they are made.

honey roll

1 egg, separated
3 egg whites
2 tablespoons treacle
½ cup (175g) golden syrup
½ cup (75g) cornflour
⅓ cup (50g) self-raising flour
1 teaspoon ground ginger
1 teaspoon ground cinnamon
½ teaspoon ground nutmeg
¼ teaspoon ground cloves
2 tablespoons boiling water
½ teaspoon bicarbonate of soda
⅓ cup (25g) desiccated coconut
mock cream
½ cup (110g) caster sugar
½ teaspoon gelatine
1 tablespoon milk
⅓ cup (80ml) water
125g butter, softened
½ teaspoon vanilla extract

1 Preheat oven to 220°C/200°C fan-assisted. Grease 25cm x 30cm swiss roll tin; line base and short sides with baking parchment, bringing paper 5cm over edges. Grease the baking parchment.
2 Beat the four egg whites in small bowl with electric mixer until soft peaks form. With motor operating, gradually add combined treacle and syrup in a thin stream.
3 Add yolk; beat until mixture is pale and thick. Transfer mixture to large bowl. Fold in triple-sifted flours and spices, and combined water and soda. Pour mixture into pan; gently spreading evenly into corners. Bake about 15 minutes.
4 Meanwhile, make mock cream.
5 Place a piece of baking parchment cut the same size as swiss roll tin on worktop; sprinkle evenly with coconut. Turn cake onto paper; peel lining paper away. Working quickly, use serrated knife to cut away crisp edges from all sides of roll.
6 Carefully roll cake loosely from one short side by lifting paper and using it to guide roll into shape; stand 10 seconds then unroll. Re-roll cake; cool to room temperature.
7 Gently unroll cake, spread with mock cream, carefully re-roll cake.
mock cream Combine sugar, gelatine, milk and water in small saucepan; stir over low heat, without boiling, until sugar and gelatine dissolve. Cool to room temperature. Beat butter and extract in small bowl with electric mixer until as white as possible. With motor operating, gradually beat in milk mixture until fluffy; this will take up to 15 minutes. Mock cream will thicken on standing.

preparation time 20 minutes
cooking time 15 minutes (plus cooling time)
serves 8

passionfruit sponge roll

3 eggs
½ cup (110g) caster sugar
1 teaspoon vanilla extract
¾ cup (100g) cornflour
¾ teaspoon cream of tartar
½ teaspoon bicarbonate of soda
¼ cup (10g) flaked coconut
¼ cup (55g) caster sugar, extra
½ cup (125ml) whipping cream
1 teaspoon icing sugar
passionfruit curd
⅓ cup (80ml) passionfruit pulp
⅔ cup (150g) caster sugar
2 eggs, beaten lightly
125g unsalted butter, chopped

1 Preheat oven to 180°C/160°C fan-assisted. Grease 25cm x 30cm swiss roll tin; line base with baking parchment, extending paper 5cm over long sides of tin.
2 Beat eggs and sugar in small bowl with electric mixer until mixture forms thick ribbons, about 8 minutes; add vanilla extract.
3 Sift cornflour, cream of tartar and bicarbonate of soda three times onto sheet of baking parchment; lightly fold into egg mixture. Pour mixture into tin, spread into corners. Sprinkle with coconut.
4 Bake for about 12 minutes or until top springs back when touched lightly.
5 Place damp tea towel on worktop. Top with sheet of baking parchment; sprinkle with extra sugar. Immediately turn sponge onto sugared paper; remove lining paper. Using serrated knife, cut away edges from short sides of sponge.
6 Roll sponge firmly from short side with paper inside; drape tea towel over roll; cool.
7 Meanwhile, make passionfruit curd.
8 Whip cream and icing sugar in small bowl with electric mixer until soft peaks form; unroll sponge, spread with half the passionfruit curd, top with cream. Roll sponge again by lifting paper and using it to guide the roll into shape.
passionfruit curd Combine ingredients in heatproof bowl; stir over pan of simmering water about 10 minutes or until thickened slightly. Cool.

preparation time 40 minutes
cooking time 25 minutes (plus cooling time)
serves 6

tips
Sponge best made on day of serving. Passion-fruit curd can be made three days ahead. Use any leftover curd as a topping for ice-cream, if desired.

chocolate roulade with coffee cream

1 tablespoon caster sugar
200g dark cooking chocolate, chopped coarsely
¼ cup (60ml) hot water
1 tablespoon instant coffee powder
4 eggs, separated
½ cup (110g) caster sugar, extra
1 teaspoon hot water, extra
300ml whipping cream
2 tablespoons coffee-flavoured liqueur
1 tablespoon icing sugar

1   Preheat oven to 180°C/160°C fan-assisted. Grease 25cm x 30cm swiss roll tin; line base with baking parchment. Place a piece of baking parchment cut the same size as swiss roll tin on worktop; sprinkle evenly with caster sugar.
2   Combine chocolate, the water and half of the coffee powder in large heatproof bowl. Stir over large saucepan of simmering water until smooth; remove from heat.
3   Beat egg yolks and extra caster sugar in small bowl with electric mixer until thick and creamy; fold egg mixture into warm chocolate mixture.
4   Meanwhile, beat egg whites in clean small bowl with electric mixer until soft peaks form; fold egg whites, in two batches, into chocolate mixture. Spread into prepared tin; bake in moderate oven about 10 minutes.
5   Turn sponge onto sugared paper, peel baking parchment away; use serrated knife to cut away crisp edges from all sides. Cover sponge with tea towel; cool.
6   Dissolve remaining coffee powder in the extra water in small bowl. Add cream, liqueur and icing sugar; beat with electric mixer until firm peaks form. Spread sponge evenly with cream mixture. Roll sponge, from long side, by lifting paper and using it to guide the roll into shape. Cover roll; refrigerate 30 minutes before serving.

preparation time 20 minutes
(plus cooling and chilling time)
cooking time 10 minutes
serves 8

tiramisu roulade

2 tablespoons coffee-flavoured liqueur
¼ cup (60ml) water
2 tablespoons caster sugar
1 tablespoon instant coffee granules
1 tablespoon boiling water
3 eggs
½ cup (110g) caster sugar, extra
½ cup (75g) plain flour
2 tablespoons flaked almonds
coffee liqueur cream
250g mascarpone cheese
½ cup (125ml) whipping cream
2 tablespoons coffee-flavoured liqueur

tip
You can use any coffee-flavoured liqueur that you prefer in the mascarpone cream filling, or try chocolate, almond or hazelnut, liquorice or mint liqueur.

1 Preheat oven to 220°C/200°C fan-assisted. Grease 25cm x 30cm swiss roll tin; line base and two long sides with baking parchment, extending paper 5cm over sides.
2 Place liqueur, the water and sugar in small saucepan; bring to the boil. Reduce heat; simmer, uncovered, without stirring, 5 minutes or until syrup thickens slightly. Remove from heat, stir in half of the coffee; reserve syrup.
3 Dissolve remaining coffee in the boiling water.
4 Beat eggs and extra sugar in small bowl with electric mixer about 5 minutes or until thick, creamy and sugar dissolves. Transfer to large bowl; fold in dissolved coffee. Fold in triple-sifted flour. Spread mixture into tin; sprinkle with almonds. Bake about 15 minutes.
5 Meanwhile, place a piece of baking parchment cut the same size as tin on worktop; sprinkle evenly with about 2 teaspoons of caster sugar. Turn sponge onto paper; peel lining paper away. Trim all sides of sponge. Using paper as guide, roll sponge from long side; cool.
6 Meanwhile, make coffee liqueur cream.
7 Unroll sponge, brush with reserved syrup; spread with cream then re-roll sponge. Cover with cling film; refrigerate 30 minutes before serving.
coffee liqueur cream Beat ingredients in small bowl with electric mixer until firm peaks form.

preparation time 35 minutes
cooking time 20 minutes (plus refrigeration time)
serves 10

glossary

almonds
blanched skins removed.
essence often interchangeable with extract; made with almond oil and alcohol or another agent.
flaked paper-thin slices.
ground also known as almond meal; nuts are powdered to a coarse flour texture.
slivered cut lengthways.
aniseed also called anise; the liquorice-flavoured seeds of the anise plant.
baking powder a raising agent containing starch, but mostly cream of tartar and bicarbonate of soda in the proportions of 1 teaspoon cream of tartar to ½ teaspoon bicarbonate of soda. This is equal to 2 teaspoons baking powder.
bicarbonate of soda also called baking soda.
bourbon authentic American whiskey originating in Bourbon County, Kentucky; made from at least 51% corn and aged in charred oak for a minimum two years.
bran, unprocessed is the coarse outer husk of cereal grains, and can be found in health food stores and supermarkets.
brazil nuts native to South America, a triangular-shelled oily nut with an unusually tender white flesh and a mild, rich flavour. Good for eating as well as cooking, the nuts can be eaten raw or cooked, or can be ground into meal for baking.
cashews plump, kidney-shaped, golden-brown nuts with a sweet, buttery flavour. Because of high fat content (48 per cent), they should be kept, sealed tightly, under refrigeration to avoid becoming rancid. We use roasted unsalted cashews in this book, unless otherwise stated.
chocolate
chips hold their shape in baking.
dark eating made of cocoa liquor, cocoa butter and sugar.

milk eating most popular eating chocolate, mild and very sweet; similar in make-up to dark, but with the addition of milk solids.
white eating contains no cocoa solids, deriving its sweet flavour from cocoa butter. Is very sensitive to heat.
chocolate hazelnut spread we use Nutella. It was originally developed when chocolate was hard to source during World War II; hazelnuts were added to extend chocolate supply.
cinnamon dried inner bark of the shoots of the cinnamon tree. Also available ground.
cloves can be used whole or in ground form. Has a strong scent and taste so should be used minimally.
cocoa powder also known as cocoa.
coconut
creamed a product made entirely from fresh coconut; sold in blocks in supermarkets.
desiccated unsweetened and concentrated, dried finely shredded.
flaked dried flaked coconut flesh.
shredded thin strips of dried coconut.
coffee and chicory essence a syrup based on sugar, caramel, coffee and chicory.
coffee-flavoured liqueur we use either Kahlua or Tia Maria coffee-flavoured liqueur.
condensed milk a canned milk product consisting of milk with more than half the water content removed and sugar added to the milk that remains.
cornflour also known as cornstarch; used as a thickening agent in cooking.
cranberries, dried have the same slightly sour, succulent flavour as fresh cranberries. Can usually be substituted for or with other dried fruit in most recipes. Available in most supermarkets. Also available in sweetened form.

cream of tartar the acid ingredient in baking powder; added to confectionery mixtures to help prevent sugar from crystallising. Keeps frostings creamy and improves volume when beating egg whites.
cream
soured a thick commercially-cultured soured cream. Minimum fat content 35%.
whipping a cream that contains a thickener. Has a minimum fat content of 35 per cent.
custard powder instant mixture used to make pouring custard; similar to North American instant pudding mixes.
date fruit of the date palm tree, eaten fresh or dried, on their own or in prepared dishes. About 4cm to 6cm in length, oval and plump, thin-skinned, with a honey-sweet flavour and sticky texture.
dulce de leche a caramel sauce made from milk and sugar. Can be used straight from the jar for cheesecakes, slices and tarts. Has similar qualities to sweetened condensed milk, only a thicker, caramel consistency; great to use in caramel desserts.
essences are synthetically produced substances used in small amounts to impart their respective flavours to foods. An extract is made by actually extracting the flavour from a food product. In the case of vanilla, pods are soaked, usually in alcohol, to capture the authentic flavour. Both extracts and essences will keep indefinitely if stored in a cool dark place.
filo pastry chilled or frozen tissue-thin pastry sheets that are very versatile, lending themselves to both sweet and savoury dishes.
flour
plain all-purpose flour.
rice extremely fine flour made from ground rice.

self-raising plain flour sifted with baking powder (a raising agent consisting mainly of 2 parts cream of tartar to 1 part bicarbonate of soda) in the proportion of 150g flour to 2 level teaspoons baking powder.

gelatine a thickening agent. Available in sheet form, known as leaf gelatine, or as a powder. Three teaspoons of dried gelatine (8g or one sachet) is roughly equivalent to four gelatine leaves.

ginger also known as green or root ginger; the thick gnarled root of a tropical plant.

stem fresh ginger root preserved in sugar syrup.

glacé cherries also known as candied cherries; boiled in heavy sugar syrup and then dried. Used in cakes, breads and sweets.

glacé fruit fruit such as cherries, peaches, pineapple, orange and citron cooked in heavy sugar syrup then dried.

golden syrup a by-product of refined sugarcane; pure maple syrup or honey can be substituted.

hazelnuts also known as filberts; plump, grape-size, rich, sweet nut having a brown inedible skin that is removed by rubbing heated nuts together vigorously in a tea-towel.

limoncello Italian lemon-flavoured liqueur; originally made from the juice and peel of lemons grown along the Amalfi coast.

macadamias native to Australia, a rich and buttery nut; store in refrigerator because of its high oil content.

maple syrup distilled from the sap of maple trees found only in Canada and parts of North America. Maple-flavoured syrup is not an adequate substitute for the real thing.

mascarpone a cultured cream product made in much the same way as yogurt. It's whitish to creamy yellow in colour, with a soft, creamy texture.

mixed peel candied citrus peel.

mixed spice a blend of ground spices usually consisting of cinnamon, allspice and nutmeg.

muesli also known as granola; a combination of grains (mainly oats), nuts and dried fruits.

nutmeg dried nut of an evergreen tree; available in ground form or you can grate your own with a fine grater.

passionfruit a small tropical fruit, native to Brazil, comprised of a tough dark-purple skin surrounding edible black sweet-sour seeds.

pecans native to the United States; golden-brown, buttery and rich. Good in savoury and sweet dishes; especially good in salads.

pepitas pale green kernels of dried pumpkin seeds; they can be bought plain or salted.

pine nuts also known as pignoli; small, cream-coloured kernels obtained from the cones of different varieties of pine trees.

pistachios pale green, delicately flavoured nut inside hard off-white shells. To peel, soak shelled nuts in boiling water about 5 minutes; drain, then pat dry.

polenta a flour-like cereal made of ground corn (maize); similar to cornmeal but finer and lighter in colour; also the name of the dish made from it.

poppy seeds Small, dried, bluish-grey seeds of the poppy plant. They have a crunchy texture and a nutty flavour. Available whole or ground in most supermarkets.

prunes commercially or sun-dried plums; store in the fridge.

rice paper edible, translucent glossy rice paper made from a dough of water combined with the pith of an Asian shrub called the rice-paper plant. Resembling a grainy sheet of, it is used in confectionery making and baking; never eat it uncooked.

rolled oats whole oat grains that have been steamed and flattened. Not the quick-cook variety.

rosewater extract made from crushed rose petals; available from health food stores and speciality grocers.

rum we prefer to use an underproof dark rum (not overproof) for a more subtle flavour.

sesame seeds black and white are the most common of these tiny oval seeds; a good source of calcium.

sugar

brown an extremely soft, fine granulated sugar retaining molasses for its deep colour and flavour.

caster also known as superfine or finely granulated table sugar.

dark brown an extremely soft, fine-grained sugar retaining the deep flavour and colour of molasses.

icing also known as confectioners' sugar or powdered sugar.

raw natural brown granulated sugar.

sunflower seeds grey-green, slightly soft, oily kernels; a nutritious snack.

treacle thick, dark syrup not unlike molasses; a by-product of sugar refining.

vanilla

pod dried long, thin pod from a tropical golden orchid grown in central and South America and Tahiti; the minuscule black seeds inside the bean are used to impart a distinctively sweet vanilla flavour.

essence obtained from vanilla beans infused in alcohol and water.

extract obtained from vanilla beans infused in water; a non-alcoholic version of essence.

walnuts as well as being a good source of fibre and healthy oils, walnuts contain a range of vitamins and minerals.

yogurt an unflavoured, full-fat cow's milk yogurt has been used in these recipes unless stated otherwise.

index

conversion charts

measures

The cup and spoon measurements used in this book are metric: one measuring cup holds approximately 250ml; one metric tablespoon holds 20ml; one metric teaspoon holds 5ml.

All cup and spoon measurements are level. The most accurate way of measuring dry ingredients is to weigh them. When measuring liquids, use a clear glass or plastic jug with the metric markings.

We use large eggs with an average weight of 60g. This book contains recipes for dishes made with raw or lightly cooked eggs. These should be avoided by vulnerable people such as pregnant and nursing mothers, invalids, the elderly, babies and young children.

dry measures

METRIC	IMPERIAL
15g	½oz
30g	1oz
60g	2oz
90g	3oz
125g	4oz (¼lb)
155g	5oz
185g	6oz
220g	7oz
250g	8oz (½lb)
280g	9oz
315g	10oz
345g	11oz
375g	12oz (¾lb)
410g	13oz
440g	14oz
470g	15oz
500g	16oz (1lb)
750g	24oz (1½lb)
1kg	32oz (2lb)

liquid measures

METRIC	IMPERIAL
30ml	1 fluid oz
60ml	2 fluid oz
100ml	3 fluid oz
125ml	4 fluid oz
150ml	5 fluid oz (¼ pint/1 gill)
190ml	6 fluid oz
250ml	8 fluid oz
300ml	10 fluid oz (½ pint)
500ml	16 fluid oz
600ml	20 fluid oz (1 pint)
1000ml (1 litre)	1¾ pints

length measures

METRIC	IMPERIAL
3mm	⅛ in
6mm	¼in
1cm	½in
2cm	¾in
2.5cm	1in
5cm	2in
6cm	2½in
8cm	3in
10cm	4in
13cm	5in
15cm	6in
18cm	7in
20cm	8in
23cm	9in
25cm	10in
28cm	11in
30cm	12in (1ft)

oven temperatures

These oven temperatures are only a guide for conventional ovens. For fan-assisted ovens, check the manufacturer's manual.

	°C (CELSIUS)	°F (FAHRENHEIT)	GAS MARK
Very low	120	250	½
Low	150	275-300	1-2
Moderately low	160	325	3
Moderate	180	350-375	4-5
Moderately hot	200	400	6
Hot	220	425-450	7-8
Very hot	240	475	9

ACP Books are published by ACP Magazines a division of PBL Media Pty Limited

Published by ACP Books, a division of ACP Magazines Ltd, 54 Park St, Sydney; GPO Box 4088, Sydney, NSW 2001. telephone (02) 9282 8618; fax (02) 9267 9438. acpbooks@acpmagazines.com.au; www.acpbooks.com.au

Printed and bound in China

United Kingdom Distributed by Australian Consolidated Press (UK), phone (01604) 642 200; fax (01604) 642 300; books@acpuk.com

A catalogue record for this book is available from the British Library

ISBN 978-1-903777-75-6

© ACP Magazines Ltd 2010

ABN 18 053 273 546

Scanpan cookware is used in the AWW Test Kitchen.

To order books:
telephone: 01604 642 200
order online: www.acpuk.com

What could be better than the wonderful aroma of a tray of
biscuits baking away in the oven? Only the knowledge that there
are lots more great ideas where they came from! From traditional
American brownies, lemon slice, chocolate chip cookies to
the perfect flapjack with syrup or honey. So easy,
to make, so easy to eat!

ISBN 978-1-903777-75-6

9 781903 777756

acp
books

UK £6.99rrp www.acpuk.com

SWEET TEMPTATIONS

The Australian Women's Weekly Home Library

✤ Cakes ✤ Ice-Creams ✤ Puddings ✤ Fruits ✤